Media Ethics Goes
to the Movies

Media Ethics Goes to the Movies

HOWARD GOOD
MICHAEL J. DILLON

PRAEGER

Westport, Connecticut
London

Library of Congress Cataloging-in-Publication Data

Good, Howard, 1951–
    Media ethics goes to the movies / Howard Good and Michael J. Dillon.
      p. cm.
    Filmography: p.
    Includes index.
    ISBN 0–275–97081–7 (alk. paper)
    1. Motion pictures—Moral and ethical aspects. I. Dillon, Michael J. II. Title.
  PN1995.5 .G66 2002
   791.43′653—dc21   2001051365

British Library Cataloguing in Publication Data is available.

Library of Congress Catalog Card Number: 2001051365
ISBN: 0–275–97081–7

First published in 2002

Praeger Publishers, 88 Post Road West, Westport, CT 06881
An imprint of Greenwood Publishing Group, Inc.
www.praeger.com

Printed in the United States of America

The paper used in this book complies with the
Permanent Paper Standard issued by the National
Information Standards Organization (Z39.48–1984).

10 9 8 7 6 5 4 3 2 1

In memory of my father-in-law, Mickey Mintzer,
who lived it.

—H. G.

To my wife, Gina, whose patience and support helped
me to complete this work; and to my mother and
father, who, by their example, taught me the value
of perseverance.

—M. D.

Contents

In the Dark:
An Introduction

All that William Boot, the protagonist of Evelyn Waugh's great satiric novel *Scoop*, knows about newspapers before he goes to work for one is what he learned in the dark from Hollywood. "He had once seen . . . a barely intelligible film about newspaper life in New York where neurotic men in shirt sleeves and eye-shades had rushed from telephone to tape machines, insulting and betraying one another in surroundings of unredeemed squalor." Of course, moviegoing isn't necessarily the best preparation for a reporting job—as Boot's subsequent misadventures in journalism demonstrate. But when used astutely in the classroom, movies can become a valuable teaching tool, a powerful lens through which to examine media professions.

Media Ethics Goes to the Movies grew out of classes taught by the authors. We compared notes and found that abstract ethical theories became vivid for our students when played out in the dramatic narrative of film. We discussed how certain movies seemed to fit perfectly with particular ethical concepts—for example, *Eight Men Out* and loyalty, or *Deadline U.S.A.* and social responsibility. After many discussions, we realized that the lessons we had taught, and the ones we had learned, offered an opportunity to collaborate on a book that might help students, teachers, and media practitioners in their quest to define and enact ethics.

Each chapter of *Media Ethics Goes to the Movies* identifies the ethical issues dramatized in a movie and outlines options for addressing them. Readers are left to decide for themselves, however, what is the right option to follow. We agree with ethicist Joel J. Kupperman, who states, "Moral progress takes place when people struggle with hard cases."

But why use movies? Lee Wilkins of the University of Missouri, Columbia, cites four reasons why she has used movies for years in teaching media ethics:

1. Movies can provide "a robust narrative" that engages the imagination and empathy of students as no textbook can.
2. Movies portray the development of relationships "over time and in a particular context," and it is relationships—with sources, colleagues, audiences, and employers—that are often at the very core of journalistic decision making.
3. Movies confront students with issues they might otherwise avoid, from war and race to professional incompetence.
4. Movies are themselves an important medium and, in a class covering "the spectrum of media," should be included.

Matthew C. Ehrlich, another journalism professor who has introduced movies-as-text into a course, notes that students are "enthusiastic about the chance to use a familiar and popular medium in learning how to think critically about their chosen profession."

As commercial products designed primarily to entertain, movies may seem destined to make ethics easy. Actually, some movies, including those analyzed here, capture human moral conduct in all its complex ambiguity. John Barton suggests in his book *Ethics and the Old Testament* that "there is something narrative can do with moral truths that cannot be done through ethical injunctions, and that is to give them what might be called an existential force." His point—and it applies as much to Hollywood movies as to biblical stories or ancient Greek myths—is that "as we become aware of the essential humanity of characters in [a] story, their underlying likeness to us . . . , the tale . . . begins to break its own frame and to illuminate the darker reaches of our own corrupt nature." Movies can be a possible source for ethics not because they present clear moral guidelines, but because they present visions of how people cope with various moral obligations and dilemmas.

Perhaps now more than ever, teenagers and young adults need to be given the opportunity to reflect on such visions. The traditional agencies of socialization—family, organized religion, schools—have seemingly lost interest in inculcating a broad sense of ethics. One youth expert comments that today's teenagers are "so undernourished ethically that it's amazing decency survives in them at all. No one has bothered to tell them the moral basics."

A recent nationwide survey of ten thousand high school students by the Josephson Institute of Ethics tends to confirm this. Ninety-two percent of the students admitted lying to their parents in the previous twelve months; 70 percent admitted cheating on an exam; 47 percent admitted stealing something from a store; 45 percent said they believe a person has to lie or cheat sometimes in order to succeed; and 36 percent said they would be willing to lie if it would help them get a good job. Michael Josephson, president of the Institute, worries about the impact of this generation entering the workforce. "They're going to be nuclear inspectors and bank auditors and legislators and mechanics," he states, "and if they bring to their workplace the same kind of attitudes revealed here, just imagine the havoc."

They are also, presumably, going to be media professionals, a role entailing serious social responsibilities. But do even current media professionals live up to their responsibilities to society? Let the distinguished media ethicist John C. Merrill answer: "If the purpose of the mass media is to water the roots of democracy by helping to create a knowledgeable and sensitive electorate, then the overabundance of sleaze, rumor, gossip, sensation, superficiality, and arrogance does not bode well for responsible journalism."

The past few years have provided frequent examples of irresponsible journalism. *Cincinnati Enquirer* reporter Mike Gallagher tapped into the voice-mail system of Chiquita Brands International and used the stolen information in an exposé of the company. NBC News secretly rigged a General Motors pickup truck to explode on impact to illustrate a story on unsafe gas tanks. Columnist Mike Barnicle resigned from the *Boston Globe* after being accused of plagiarism and fabrication. And, perhaps worst of all, a circus atmosphere prevailed whenever the media descended en masse on an event, be it the O. J. Simpson trial, the death of Princess Diana, or the shootings at Columbine High School.

Small wonder the reputation of the press for honesty and integrity, never very strong in the best of times, is even weaker than usual today. Survey after survey reveals a public disgusted with the press's performance. A 1998 poll by the Freedom Forum found that 88 percent of respondents believe that reporters use unethical or illegal means to get stories, while another poll the same year by the American Society of Newspaper Editors (ASNE) found that 80 percent think that journalists sensationalize stories to sell more papers.

It isn't uncommon for journalists to try and shift the blame for the so-called tabloidization of the media back onto the public. "What about the hypocrisy of the viewers and the readers?" pundit Michael Kinsley asks. "They say they don't like us; they're disgusted with the press for covering all the sleaze, and then they create a market for it." But even if the press is simply giving audiences what they want, is that ethical? Aren't journalists bound by philosophy and tradition to aim for something higher? Why extend them the constitutional protection of the First Amendment if all they are going to do with it is put on a circus?

Working journalists rarely reflect on these kinds of questions. Their attention is taken up by more practical matters, from the phone numbers of sources to the deadlines for stories. Ethics is relegated to the idealistic world of books, speeches, roundtable discussions, and classrooms. But ethical behavior is a necessity, not a luxury. In its simplest and most profound terms, ethics is about how we treat each other. Or, as Aristotle said, "All virtue is summed up in dealing justly."

The media possess immense power for good or ill. With family life in decay and schools in crisis, and with the pace of social change accelerating, people increasingly rely on the media to tell them what to think, say, and do. We live in an around-the-clock, pedal-to-the-metal Media Nation—under Microsoft, indivisible, with tabloid television and sports radio for all. If we are to survive the rush and roar, it is no longer enough for media professionals to be technically proficient. They must also be morally informed.

COMING ATTRACTIONS

Like nearly everything else in this book, our choice of which movies to analyze is open to second-guessing. Some might expect that a book with the declamatory title *Media Ethics Goes to the Movies* would include for analysis only movies directly about the media. But that isn't the case. Readers will find a baseball picture, a courtroom drama, and a violent action flick among the movies analyzed here.

The explanation is simple: Despite featuring ballplayers, jurors, or commandos, these movies raise the kinds of ethical issues that haunt media professionals.

What other factors went into our movie choices? Perhaps the most important was that the movies present morally ambiguous situations. This let out movies like *The Sweet Smell of Success* (1957) and *Absence of Malice* (1981), which deal with media ethics, but in stark, black-and-white terms. There is never any doubt in viewers' minds that the reporter in *Absence of Malice* or the press agent in *The Sweet Smell of Success* are thoroughly unscrupulous. In the movies we chose to include, the line between hero and villain, right and wrong, is harder to discern, and requiring sustained moral reflection.

Chapters 1 and 2 examine the classic newspaper movies *Ace in the Hole* (1951) and *Deadline U.S.A.* (1952), respectively. *Ace in the Hole* (also known as *The Big Carnival*) portrays a public as eager to have its emotions manipulated as the press is to manipulate them. Although the movie was too corrosive to be a hit when first released, its portrayal of a wildly ambitious reporter who creates a media spectacle out of a trivial mine cave-in now seems prophetic.

In chapter 2, *Deadline U.S.A.* inspires a discussion about whether journalists can behave ethically in the face of corporate practices and objectives beyond their personal control. A managing editor—played snarlingly here by movie tough guy Humphrey Bogart—insists that his newspaper live up to its moral obligations even as it is put on the auction block. Such issues have grown in significance over the past fifty years as newspapers have died, merged, or been absorbed by communication conglomerates. The chapter explores this trend against the backdrop of the social responsibility theory of the press, which was articulated in the Hutchins Commission report, released contemporaneously with the movie.

Chapter 3 uses *All the President's Men* (1976), a paranoid thriller about the Watergate scandal, to explore the relation of means to ends. It asks whether the two young *Washington Post* reporters played by Dustin Hoffman and Robert Redford are justified in invading privacy, coercing sources, and misrepresenting themselves in order to expose corruption at the highest levels of the American government. The answer of some philosophers may surprise you.

In chapter 4, readers are introduced to the protagonists of *Under Fire* (1983), a tight little band of correspondents and photojournalists who rove from one murderous third world conflict to another, like tourists in hell. The movie raises questions about the morality of the Western press profiting from the horrors of war. It also affords an opportunity to discuss certain responsibilities peculiar to photojournalists. For example, to whom are photojournalists primarily responsible, the subjects of their photographs or the viewers of them?

Chapter 5 applies a decision-making model called the Potter Box to the various personal and professional crises faced by characters in *The Paper* (1994), a movie about a typically frantic day in the life of a New York City tabloid. Editors clash with reporters and each other over what stories to run and how and when to run them. With the help of the Potter Box, readers may reason their way through these decisions better than the characters in the movie do.

The setting shifts from the newsroom to the courtroom in chapter 6 and then to the ballpark in chapter 7. Both chapters, though, continue the book's focus on issues pertinent to media professionals. Chapter 6 analyzes the long drawn-out deliberations of the all-male jury in *12 Angry Men* (1957), with the purpose of illustrating the elusiveness of facts and the uncertainty of perceptions—matters that journalists, professionally obligated to be fair and accurate, must somehow resolve.

Chapter 7 takes readers out to the ball game, where disgruntled White Sox players in *Eight Men Out* (1988) conspire with gamblers to throw the World Series. The chapter traces possible parallels between the players and journalists. Can either ever justify cheating on the job? Do both have a responsibility to use their talent to the fullest, regardless of what the market demands? These are just a couple of the difficult questions the chapter asks.

With chapter 8, the book returns to a more direct examination of media ethics. Readers meet Steve Everett, the down-at-the-heels reporter played with a kind of bewildered misery by Clint Eastwood in *True Crime* (1999). Everett, whose boozing and womanizing have wrecked his once-illustrious career, stumbles onto a story that can save an innocent man from the execution chamber. As the chapter follows his ragged efforts to prevent a miscarriage of justice, it confirms the distinction Aristotle drew between the morally evil person and the morally weak one. It also favorably compares W. D. Ross's duty-based ethics with utilitarianism, which has been described as "the news media's predominant mode of moral reasoning."

Chapter 9 uses *Network*, a caustic satire from 1976, to explore just how far media ownership might go to reap profits. The film depicts television executives willing to do almost anything, including staging terrorist attacks and on-air murders, for the sake of higher ratings. If this reminds you of the so-called reality programing that dominates TV today—shows like *Survivor*, *The Mole*, and *Temptation Island*—it is because *Network* grasps the fact that modern mass media commodify human experience, transforming life into for-profit entertainment.

The exploration of the dark side of entertainment continues with chapter 10. Focusing on a typical action movie, *The Rock* (1996), the chapter sifts through the factors that contribute to the dehumanizing effects of entertainment violence on viewers. This ultimately leads to a discussion of whether society has a stake in controlling media portrayals of violence and, if so, the best form for control to take.

It is time now to dim the lights all the way: Coming attractions are over. If a favorite movie or subject of yours has been omitted, we plead in defense that this is a book, not a library—there is only room for so much. And, in any case, we believe that what is included here has broad application. Ethics is ethics, whether you are in front of the camera or on a copy desk, whether you shoot video or write press releases, whether you are pursuing a career in news or advertising or entertainment. To be an ethical professional at anything, you must first be an ethical person.

We offer this book in hopes that it will contribute in some small way to the ethical growth of the young people entering the media professions. There is a concept in Judaism called *tikkun olam*, which is Hebrew for "repairing the world." According to the concept, human beings have not only the ability, but also an obligation to fix the problems of society—from violence and hate to greed, disease, poverty, and injustice. While the problems may be too large and complex for any one person to solve, each of us can do a part. This book is ours. The question is, What will be yours?

FURTHER READING

Barton, John. *Ethics and the Old Testament*. Harrisburg, Penn.: Trinity, 1998.

Edmond, Patricia. "America's Escalating Honesty Crisis." *USA Weekend*, 16–18, October 1998, 14–15.

Ehrlich, Matthew C. "Thinking Critically about Journalism through Popular Culture." *Journalism Educator* (Winter 1996): 35–41.

Jones, Rebecca. "Looking for Goodness." *American School Board Journal* (December 1998): 14–19.

Kupperman, Joel J. *Character*. New York: Oxford University Press, 1991.
Merrill, John C. *Journalism Ethics: Philosophical Foundations for News Media*. New York: St. Martin's, 1997.
Waugh, Evelyn. *Scoop*. Boston: Little, Brown, 1937.
Wilkins, Lee. "Film As Ethics Text." *Journal of Mass Media Ethics* (Spring–Summer 1987): 109–113.
———. "Why Take Your Ethics Class to the Movies?" *Ethical News* (Winter 1999): 7.

1

Ace in the Hole:
The Dark Side of the Force

Despite committing almost every journalistic sin imaginable—including a few before the opening credits have even finished scrolling—Kirk Douglas's oily and opportunistic newsman Chuck Tatum in Billy Wilder's 1951 film *Ace in the Hole* nevertheless articulates the essence of ethical decision making. Locked in a struggle with an impossibly pure small-town editor for the soul of a naïve cub reporter, Tatum snarls, "Everybody in this game has to make up his own mind."

Indeed, despite working within an often-confining web of institutional rules and social expectations, journalists must ultimately take responsibility for their actions. But, as *Ace in the Hole* points out, so too must media managers and audience members. When members of the press and public abdicate their personal responsibilities and fail to anticipate the consequences of their actions, the human and moral costs can be exorbitant.

In an age of urbanization and mass politics, it is the media that serve as the nexus of community conversation and action. Democratic theory is predicated on a marketplace of ideas where rational people convene to debate their collective destiny; today, with face-to-face politics a practical impossibility, it is the media that serve as a symbolic town square. The First Amendment singles out the press for special protection from state persecution because the framers of the Constitution recognized that without a free press, there could be no free and open civic conversation. That special protection, therefore, comes with an implied responsibility to work in the public interest. That is why no journalism education is complete without a strong ethical grounding. Philosopher Sissela Bok's contention that honoring public trust is a paramount goal of ethical decision making in any endeavor is especially germane to journalism.

Ace in the Hole (AKA *The Big Carnival*) is one of the most withering portraits of the American news media and its audience ever produced by Hollywood. The film presents an ideal vehicle for an exploration of how journalists navigate—or, in this case, create—ethical minefields. It does so against a backdrop of the personal, institutional, and social relationships that guide and delimit the work of reporters. It also offers many fruitful avenues for discussions about the roles, ethos, and methods of journalism.

Ace in the Hole appeared amid a spate of flag-waving celebrations of the American press. *Deadline U.S.A.* (see chapter 2) was released the same year and portrayed an American press that fought valiantly against destructive market forces and organized crime. *Call Northside 777*, released in 1948, chronicled the dogged efforts of a hero-reporter to use the press's power as a court of last resort to bring justice to a man wrongly imprisoned for murder.

Director Billy Wilder's mediascape, however, is populated by greedy, hypercompetitive publishers, reporters who place intense personal ambition far ahead of the public interest, and a public of willing spectators who are as eager to have their emotions manipulated as the press is to manipulate them. That dance of manipulation between journalist and audience is at the heart of *Ace in the Hole*. The more brazenly Tatum stage-manages the rescue attempt of a simple-minded cave explorer, the more mawkish his audience's reactions become.

A LOAF OF BREAD WITH A FILE IN IT

The plot of *Ace in the Hole* is Dantesque. A hard-bitten Gotham reporter who has gambled, boozed, and philandered his way out of the big time hits rock bottom while driving through Albuquerque, New Mexico (portrayed as one of the lower rungs of journalistic hell).

Both Tatum and his car have broken down when he strolls into the offices of the local newspaper and tries to con kindly editor Jacob Q. Boot (Porter Hall) into hiring him. Tatum guarantees the editor a profit of $200 per week. "I'm a $250 a week newspaper man," Tatum declares. "I can be had for $50." Booth, a man so cautious that he wears a belt *and* suspenders, agrees to give Tatum a tryout.

Tatum begins to wonder if the big story he needs—"a loaf of bread with a file in it"—will ever materialize. But after a year of covering jerkwater small-town news stories—all the while fantasizing about "a good trunk murder," a catastrophe at nearby Los Alamos, or, better still, a rattlesnake rampage—Tatum finds his springboard back to the big leagues. Accompanied by neophyte reporter and photographer Herbie Cook (Robert Arthur), Tatum is on his way to yet another mundane news event when he stumbles into a dramatic human interest story that will sizzle over the wires to New York—with Tatum figuring to trail triumphantly behind, of course.

Opportunity presents itself in the form of Leo Minosa, a former serviceman with the faith, and intellect, of a child. Tatum finds Minosa trapped in an old Indian cliff dwelling, where he has been searching for artifacts in the quixotic hope that by striking it rich he can win the esteem and affection of his peroxide-blonde wife, Lorraine Minosa (Jan Sterling). Pushing aside a blustering deputy who can see no possibility for personal gain by risking his own hide to help Leo Minosa, Tatum quickly organizes a rescue and begins to plot his return to prominence.

While Minosa wheezes and prays in the tomb he has fashioned through his own foolishness, Tatum, Lorraine, corrupt local sheriff Gus Kretzer (Ray Teal), and malleable mining engineer Sam Smollett (Frank Jaquet) create a virtual synergy of cynicism that will bring thousands of "fans" to the remote cave dwelling and enthrall a nation following Minosa's struggle in newspapers and on radio and television.

Instead of shoring up tunnels and pulling Minosa out—a twelve-hour job—Tatum convinces the authorities that it is to everyone's advantage (except Minosa's, of course) to drill a rescue shaft from the top of the mountain. The rescue will be visually dramatic and, more importantly, take an entire week—enough time to create a full-blown media frenzy.

For one week, the sheriff, who is up for reelection, will have a forum to woo voters. For one week, Lorraine Minosa, who refuses to pray for her husband—"kneeling bags my nylons," she tartly explains—will make a fortune selling food, gas, and parking spaces to curious mobs. For one week, Tatum will have an exclusive story (Sheriff Kretzer sees to it that all competing reporters are denied access to the rescue scene) that will allow him to write his own ticket back to New York.

And for one week, Leo Minosa, who sees Tatum as both friend and savior, who is proud of the grief he is sure his wife feels, and who is moved to tears that thousands of strangers have come to witness his struggle, will lie with his legs pinned in a damp cave while the incessant pounding of the drill sends clouds of gritty dust into his failing lungs.

By the end of the week, a virtual city has sprung up outside of the cave dwelling. A carnival, complete with a Ferris wheel, infuses gaiety into the proceedings, and a local country and western band scores with a hastily penned ode to Leo Minosa. It is, quite literally, a media circus.

Wilder's prescient film seems a dress rehearsal for the overwrought media treatment of Princess Diana's death four decades later. In fact, *Ace in the Hole* itself was inspired by the real-life media spectacle that accompanied the unsuccessful rescue attempt of Kentucky cave explorer Floyd Collins twenty-five years earlier. That story brought a Pulitzer Prize to *Louisville Courier* reporter "Skeets" Miller, who, in addition to his considerable reporting skills, had the good fortune to possess a slight enough build to crawl down a shaft to interview Collins as he lay dying. The Collins story was the first to create a national sensation via the new medium of radio broadcasting.

Tatum's grandiose plan to create a sensational media event in which he as much as Minosa will star goes awry, however. As Tatum builds suspense and fascination in his daily dispatches, Minosa's health fades and it becomes obvious that death is sure to beat the drill. Worse, the drill's incessant pounding has so weakened the cave's tunnels that the first—and easiest—option for rescuing Minosa is foreclosed. In the end, Minosa dies, Tatum misses his deadline, which is scooped by ravenous, gloating competitors, and the disappointed crowd disperses in a cloud of desert dust, leaving Minosa's devout and helpless parents to mourn amid a landscape of litter and cast-off carnival trappings. Tatum himself ends up with a mortal stab wound, courtesy of Lorraine, but redeems himself before dying by ignoring his own wound and bringing a priest to give Minosa the last rites of his Catholic faith.

A GRIM ALLEGORY

Ace in the Hole is best understood as an allegory in which the key characters personify social and political institutions. Tatum represents the dark, sensational journalism that has steadily gained ascendance in the twentieth century. Booth represents the ideals of journalism—he is socially responsible, careful, and temperate. The sheriff represents the government; his relationship with Tatum raises questions about the often overly cozy relationship between state power and journalism. Federber (Frank Cady), who is the first tourist to arrive on the scene of the rescue, embodies a public fascinated with media spectacle. Minosa, like many news subjects who find themselves unexpectedly in the spotlight, is fatally unaware of the vast machinery that will transform his personal struggle into a public commodity. He is akin to the shadow in Plato's cave, and Tatum's audience members are like Plato's prisoner, dependent on the journalist to present an image of the world in which they must act. Like many others caught in the spotlight's glare, Minosa finds himself honored despite his dire situation. He perks up and wipes three layers of grime from his face when Tatum tells him he plans to write a story about Minosa and publish his picture. "My picture?" Minosa asks in awe. "Honest? How do you like that? Me in the paper!"

Tatum's constant companion in his machinations to push the Leo Minosa story into the national limelight is Herbie Cook, a wide-eyed cub reporter whom Tatum seduces into his cynical world. The relationship between Tatum and Cook is especially important to an ethical analysis of *Ace in the Hole*. In a sense, Cook represents every young aspiring journalist whose methods and worldview will be shaped largely by the models he chooses.

Tatum gradually draws Cook away from the virtuous, but plodding, Booth and offers him a virtual primer in the ways of media manipulation. The conflict over Cook's soul is as old as literature (Christ's wanderings in the desert as the devil tempts him), as well as a staple of genre film (Obi Wan's struggle with Darth Vader to save Luke Skywalker from the dark side of the Force). Cook's slide into the seamy world of sensational journalism offers an enticing and intriguing vehicle to explore the process by which young journalists formulate a moral code.

MENTORS AND MODELS

Aristotle observed that by choosing a virtuous model, an individual can begin to build a strong moral foundation. A young journalist who values ethics would do well to identify an older reporter who embodies moral traits.

In *Ace in the Hole*, Cook is torn between loyalty to Booth and to Tatum, who exudes power and excitement. Aspiring reporters face the same choices today. The most prominent journalists are not always the most ethical. For television news personalities, especially, the need to construct and maintain a public image can overwhelm the stories they cover. Asking "tough" questions has become a part of long-time ABC correspondent Sam Donaldson's persona, and audiences expect a "tough" performance when he appears on television. This is not to say that Donaldson is an unethical journalist, but his reputation can actually distract the audience from the public issues he is covering; in essence, his persona demands that he perform in a certain way whether that is the best way to get the news or not.

Philosophers disagree about the definition of ethics and the best way to practice ethical behavior. But no philosopher has ever posited that celebrity is tantamount to virtue. Young reporters seeking models have to look beyond the obvious choices to identify experienced journalists who possess effective newsgathering methods and ethical traits even if, like Booth, they turn out to be dogged rather than charismatic. In *Ace in the Hole*, Tatum's charisma blinds Cook to his unscrupulous methods.

It is a central paradox of the film that the cold and ruthless Tatum has an unerring instinct for stirring up the emotions of his audience. Even the flinty-hearted Lorraine is astonished by Tatum's audacity, observing, "I've met a lot of hard-boiled eggs in my life, but you're 20 minutes." And it is ironic that despite Tatum's seamy motives, he gives the hapless Minosa his only real chance at life; without the intercession of publicity, no civic authority would have lifted a finger to help.

Minosa's transformation from inept cave explorer to media martyr raises a profound question about the "human interest" function of news: By turning human experience into drama and entertainment, does journalism tap into our sense of humanity, or does it encourage us to divest ourselves of it in the pursuit of selfish emotional gratification? Reporters naturally see the world in terms of narrative potential, but this peculiar vision can cause them to perceive the subjects of their stories in strictly instrumental ways. In *Ace in the Hole*, Tatum clearly sees Minosa primarily as an instrument that can be used to construct a spellbinding story and further his own career. He conceives of Minosa as a type, as the raw material for a compelling narrative, and fails to recognize Minosa's humanity until it is too late.

The professional standards of journalism in essence give reporters a checklist they can use to evaluate the newsworthiness of occurrences; there are an infinite number of occurrences in the world every day, but relatively few are deemed worth reporting. How do reporters decide which events possess the right "ingredients" to make them worthy of publicity? Newsworthy events are those events that possess timeliness, proximity, conflict, drama, human interest, public consequence, celebrity, or unusualness. The more of these elements an event possesses, the more newsworthy it is likely to be. In pleading for a job, Tatum promises Booth that he will go to any lengths to get the news, "and if there's no news, I'll go out and bite a dog."

Journalists are also encouraged to adopt ethical standards, but these standards, except when backed by institutional policies, are largely voluntary; everyone indeed "has to make up his [or her] own mind." Generally speaking, journalists are required by the prevailing professional norm of objectivity to keep personal and political biases out of their stories. Reporters are expected to honestly represent themselves; that is, to practice the ethical principle of disclosure as they gather information. They are expected to be scrupulously accurate and resist the temptation to embellish or invent (indeed, Tatum is greatly amused by a crocheted sign in Booth's office that reads, "Tell the Truth"). They are urged not to interfere in the playing out of the events they cover. They are expected to avoid conflicts of interest—that is, covering stories where personal, professional, or economic prerequisites are at stake. They are urged to consider the privacy and dignity of the people they write about. They are urged to bring a sense of proportion to the overall news report.

The story Tatum encounters in *Ace in the Hole* is chock-full of news elements. It is dramatic and suspenseful—will the drill or the reaper win the race for Minosa? It is unusual and bizarre, especially given that Minosa believes his fate has been caused by ancient Indian spirits upset that graves have been disturbed. The human interest inherent in the story is intense. In practical terms, whether Minosa lives or dies is of little consequence to the larger public.

Few ethical guidelines are considered in the pursuit of the Leo Minosa story. The shrill presentation of the story creates a frenzy, which then becomes part of the story. Minosa and his family are stripped of any privacy as hordes rush to the scene. The exploitation of Minosa's superstitions, which he begs Tatum to keep in confidence, leaves him with little dignity. In embellishing the superstitious angle of the story and keeping secret the bargain that has led to Minosa's prolonged imprisonment, Tatum obviously violates principles of accuracy and noninterference. And in highlighting Minosa's story over all others, many of which have far greater social consequence, Tatum and all of the news organizations printing his stories—including Booth's—lose all sense of proportion.

While the ethical violations in *Ace in the Hole* are writ large, consider news stories currently in the headlines. At what points do news values and ethical duties collide? What is the implied rationale behind each story? What would you do if you were faced with a conflict between compelling professional objectives and ethical duties?

WHERE ANGELS FEAR TO TREAD

One way to understand the larger ethical dynamics portrayed in *Ace in the Hole* is to employ established ethical models. Kim B. Rotzoll points out, "The purpose of sound moral reasoning is to draw responsible conclusions that yield justifiable results." The phrase "moral reasoning" is central to an understanding of ethics because ethical judgments require both a commitment to moral outcomes *and* intellectual honesty and rigor; good intentions are not enough. A wide variety of ethical models and maxims have been applied to journalism. This chapter uses four models as prisms through which the numerous ethical pitfalls of *Ace in the Hole* can be explored—Aristotle's Golden Mean, Immanuel Kant's Categorical Imperative, John Stuart Mill's Utilitarianism, and John Rawls's Veil of Ignorance.

Each model emphasizes a distinct process and set of objectives for ethical action. Aristotle emphasizes moderation. Kant is concerned with the establishment of universal laws (analogous in some ways to civic, professional, and institutional policies). Mill is concerned with discovering and enhancing the common good. Rawls emphasizes empathy. These models are particularly germane to a discussion of journalism ethics because the principles embedded in each are the ones most commonly used—and misused—by journalists when they explain or defend their work.

Journalists often invoke ethical principles *after* they have made their decisions, and usually only in the face of public criticism. For instance, in the aftermath of its publication of the notorious "Boston

Photographs" by Stanley Foreman—which showed a woman falling to her death from a fire escape—the managers of the *Boston Herald* invoked Utilitarian principles. By publishing the photos, the *Herald* argued, the newspaper was creating public awareness of hazardous fire escapes and therefore serving the greater good. There is no evidence, however, that in the hours that led up to publication anyone at the *Herald* reflected on the possible benefits or drawbacks of publishing the pictures. They were just vivid, sensational pictures and met many of the standards of newsworthiness described earlier. More telling, the *Herald* did not make any sustained effort after the tragedy to investigate the condition of fire escapes in the city or use its editorial pages to crusade for more thorough inspections.

Similarly in 1983 when *USA Today* disclosed, against his wishes, that tennis star Arthur Ashe had AIDS, it explained, under the glare of angry readers, that it had operated according to the Aristotelian principles of moderation by giving Ashe time to inform his family before breaking the story (instead of just running it immediately) and to Utilitarian principles by invoking the public benefits of telling Ashe's story. In one of the more audacious rationalizations offered by the press, *USA Today* editor Peter Pritchard explained that even though Ashe had been dragged unwillingly into the public spotlight at a moment of extreme vulnerability, "by sharing his story Arthur Ashe and his family are free of great weight. In the days ahead, they will help us better understand AIDS and how to defeat it."

In neither case did the news organizations or individual decision makers meet Rotzoll's standard of ethical rigor. There is little evidence that news managers debated the public interest as they prepared their stories, therefore it cannot be said that their conclusions—whether "right" or "wrong"—were truly responsible. Nor could they truly justify their actions when public ire was aroused. Unable to offer sincere, ethically grounded justifications for their actions, they used ethical principles post facto as rationalizations to mollify critics. As Homer observed, "Even a fool may be wise after the event."

No one who has not gone through the hard work of reflection and introspection about what his or her ethical principles and goals are can really make an "ethical" decision on the spot. A deadline decision may indeed turn out to have social benefits, but unless the reporter or editor encountered the situation with a well-thought-out ethical code already in place, such benefits are by nature accidental.

ETHICAL KEYSTONES

Aristotle's ethics are based on moderation. According to Aristotle, when confronted with an ethical dilemma, an individual must imagine a spectrum of possible action. The extreme ends of the spectrum will usually prove unwise or unvirtuous. Therefore, a decision maker must try to discover the Golden Mean—that is, the action between the extremes that serves justice. For instance, a man who encounters a wreck on the highway in which the driver has been critically injured has many options: go for help, try to provide assistance and comfort, or flee and let someone else worry about it. If our potential good Samaritan knows cardiopulmonary resuscitation (CPR) and help is far away, the obvious choice is to provide assistance. If, however, he does not know CPR, it would be well intentioned but foolish to try to provide aid he is not really capable of providing. Fleeing is certainly not a moral option. Therefore, the action that represents the Golden Mean would be for the rescuer to provide what comfort he could and then make a dash for life-saving help.

Aristotle's ethics are not, however, based on middling compromise. It takes imagination and creativity to clearly discover the possible spectrum of action. And the "mean" does not necessarily mean the middle. We must use our intellects to creatively consider the options available to us rather than simplistically framing our actions between two obvious choices. In our example of the critically injured motorist, the passerby untrained in first aid might demonstrate virtuous good intentions by attempting to give assistance instead of running away. But the decision is ultimately an unethical one. Going for help gives the victim the best chance to live.

Despite his cynicism, Tatum tries to justify his actions throughout the film in an attempt to persuade others to aid in his plan—and to salve his own conscience. He misuses the idea of the Golden Mean as a rationale to defend his decision to keep Minosa—his "ace in the hole"—trapped for a week instead of a day. Tatum reasons that without his intercession, Minosa would have died anyway and frames the spectrum of possibilities this way: Let Minosa die by not interceding, or let him die by prolonging his captivity indefinitely. Tatum's "mean"—which is hardly golden—is to let Minosa languish only for as long as it takes to make the story big enough to garner national attention.

Mill's theory of social utility exhorts decision makers to choose the path that leads to "the greatest good for the greatest number." For instance, when doctors are faced with a large-scale disaster, such as an airplane crash, they perform triage by first treating patients with the greatest chance to survive instead of more critically ill victims whose care would be more time-consuming and less certain.

This ethical model is central to journalism, which is charged with helping to determine the greater good in a world of endless options. The model is often misused, however. For a callow journalist, Mill's exhortation to choose "the greatest good" can be interpreted selfishly to support almost any action. Tatum reasons that prolonging Minosa's captivity and creating a media sensation serves a number of beneficial ends.

The money his wife makes exploiting the crowd will give Minosa a nest egg with which to build a better life. The public, meanwhile, will be served by experiencing an emotional catharsis that will reaffirm their humanity. It's the 1950s. People everywhere are living under the threat of the atomic bomb. There is a war in Korea. Inhumanity, it seems, is everywhere, but as Tatum explains to Cook, it is so overwhelming and involves so many victims that readers cannot begin to fathom it on an emotional level.

With one individual to focus on, audience members can feel a real emotional resonance that allows them to unleash and experience their emotions—fear, pity, compassion, and an urge to help. Tatum recalls Josef Stalin's dictum that "a million deaths is a statistic, but one death is a tragedy," when he explains to Cook that readers cannot become emotionally engaged with stories about large-scale losses of life. "One man is different, you want to know all about him. Somebody all by himself like Lindbergh crossing the Atlantic or Floyd Collins . . . that's human interest."

When Cook is taken aback that Tatum could want Minosa to remain trapped for an entire week, Tatum feigns indignation. Invoking the professional standard of journalistic noninterference, he explains that he is a mere conduit between an occurrence and an audience eager to know more about it. "I'm not wishing for anything," Tatum explains. "I don't make things happen. All I do is write about them." This is nonsense. Clearly, Tatum is the one making things happen as the "rescue" progresses.

The publicity that Tatum confers on Minosa does benefit him in some direct ways. After arriving on the scene, Tatum threatens the authorities with exposure if they do not make an effort to rescue Minosa. The threat of negative publicity can act as a powerful spur to official action. Journalism is called the Fourth Estate because it is supposed to act as a watchdog, alerting the public when elected officials evade or fail in their responsibilities.

The public confers the responsibility for the use of public resources on its elected officials. The authorities, therefore, have a moral obligation to use public resources to benefit the public and its individual members. At the outset of *Ace in the Hole*, Sheriff Kretzer cannot be bothered with Minosa because it will take him away from a community gathering where there are sure to be voters. This is a selfish use of his public authority and a clear sign to the scheming Tatum that the sheriff can easily be enlisted in his corrupt plan to hype Minosa's rescue (the fact that the sheriff keeps a rattlesnake for a pet certainly serves as another clue).

Tatum points out that a sensational story will draw intense media attention that will be far more politically powerful than a face-to-face gathering. "You play along with me and I'll have you reelected," he promises the sheriff. "You don't and I'll crucify you."

The press has no "official powers." The protections of the First Amendment, the right to examine public documents, and the right to question official decisions are available to all citizens. The press's social and political power springs from its ability to amplify its voice, influence citizens, and set an agenda for public discourse. In essence, reporters are public surrogates, or "professional citizens." They exercise the powers of citizenship on behalf of others who have neither the time nor the means to do so.

Coercion would seem to violate the spirit of ethical decision making. But Tatum's initial decision to coerce the sheriff into helping Minosa by invoking the legitimate threat of negative publicity does serve the greater good because it ensures that public resources—in this case, the authority and money to initiate a rescue—will be used appropriately. However, there is no greater social benefit in prolonging Minosa's rescue. Nor is the larger good served by Tatum's false depiction of the sheriff as a courageous leader.

It is immoral for the press and the state to deprive an individual of his life or liberty to enhance power and profits. In this case, public resources are squandered on an unnecessarily expensive rescue, and the political system is tainted by the elevation of Sheriff Kretzer to hero. Tatum starts off on the right track, but finishes beyond the ethical pale.

Where Aristotle advises moderation and Mill seeks "the greatest good," Kant urges decision makers to adopt "universal maxims."

That means that before we commit to a course of action we must agree to take the same course of action in all similar circumstances in the future. Most news organizations, for instance, do not name women who make rape allegations, but do name men accused of rape. What happens, though, when it becomes obvious that a woman alleging rape cannot prove her case? Kant would insist that once a "universal maxim" or policy has been established, there can be no exceptions. Even a person who makes an unsubstantiated accusation should not be identified.

Kant, at first, might appear to be the ultimate bureaucrat, binding the world with laws and rules. Kant's ethics, however, can be read in a cautionary light. If we knew that a decision would lead to a universal law that could never be excepted, we would be very careful about the policies we made. A true Kantian makes decisions carefully, always mindful that what seems to make good sense today might create injustice tomorrow.

The central characters in *Ace in the Hole* are only too willing to invoke established policies when those policies are in their own self-interest, but quickly abandon them when a different course of action seems more profitable. Mining engineer Sam Smollett is an excellent case in point. He is one of the film's more sympathetic figures, a decent, honest man who is appalled by the notion that Minosa's suffering should be extended in order to create political gain for the sheriff and prestige for Tatum. Good mining principles, he explains, dictate that Minosa must be rescued by using timbers to shore up the cave's tunnels so that rescuers will have safe passage to the chamber where Minosa lies injured. He knows the drilling idea is preposterous and immoral. However, when the sheriff threatens to cut him out of county work projects, Smollett abandons his "Kantian principles" and signs on for the drill rescue.

True belief in a principle means that the principle is bigger than the fate of the individual who holds it. That is why a maxim of the judicial system is that the United States is "a nation of laws, not men." Fidelity to a principle implies a willingness to act according to the dictates of that principle no matter the consequences. Rather than exposing the plot to keep Minosa trapped and appealing for public support for the more efficient rescue, the mining engineer abandons his principles to spare himself the sheriff's retribution.

Rawls's ethical model is called the Veil of Ignorance. "Justice emerges," Rawls argues, "when negotiating without social differentiation." Rawls's model is, of course, metaphorical. Faced with a decision, each actor involved must step behind the veil, where their personal and official identities will be shed. They must accept the fact that they might emerge from behind the veil in a very different role. When judge and prisoner step behind the veil, they might emerge with roles reversed. Would the judge find his sentence just if he were to fill the shoes of the prisoner? Extending empathy might well temper his administration of justice. The sensibility behind the Veil of Ignorance can be seen at work in corporate training on issues such as sexual harassment. Trainers often employ role-playing to help male managers understand the point of view of female subordinates.

While the exercise of empathy is at the center of Rawls's model, it can be more fully understood in light of Kant's ethics. A Kantian accepts that any precedent he establishes can lead to a policy that might well at some point be applied to him. Rawls urges us to understand that while we may hold the advantages in a situation today, we might not tomorrow. If, through honest reflection, Tatum, Sheriff Kretzer, and Smollett stepped behind the Veil of Ignorance, they might find themselves at the end of the process trapped in the cave. Would they really consent to a prolonged rescue? Or would the value of an individual's life take on greater value than someone else's professional or political objectives?

Tatum seems to genuinely like Minosa, even as he plots to keep him imprisoned in the cave. But his primary conception of Minosa is as a news subject; Minosa's humanity takes a back seat to his narrative potential. Only when it becomes apparent that Minosa is doomed does Tatum abandon his scheme and consider Minosa as a real and valuable human being. At the end of the film, by attempting to truly help Minosa escape at the expense of his carefully planned story, Tatum begins the practice of real empathy rather than the synthetic creation of it for public consumption.

Empathy is an oft-misunderstood concept because it is frequently confused with sympathy and is seen as an almost indulgent emotion. For journalists, the practice of empathy should be more than a simple check on conscience. A reporter's duty is to understand the meanings and implications of the stories he or she writes. Empathy is not simply a form of compassion. It requires intellectual rigor; to understand the perspectives of diverse actors in a story—as they understand them—is to understand the story better as well.

Only through a willingness to understand the motivations and points of view of conflicting sources in a story can a reporter truly understand the full dimensions of the story. Therefore, it is not an ethical betrayal to listen carefully to and try to understand, say, a prisoner you are interviewing. The exercise of empathy does not imply approval. It simply commits a reporter to postpone judgment until all of the facts are known and understood.

In *Ace in the Hole*, empathy is central not only to the actors who will determine Minosa's fate, but also to the relationship between the news media and the crowd that gathers at the cave dwelling. Federber, a vacationing insurance salesman who is the first spectator to stumble onto the scene of the rescue, personifies the crowd that rapidly gathers. Why is he there? He claims that empathy and a wish to provide moral support to Minosa have guided his actions. He can imagine how awful it must be to be trapped in a cave. His claim to empathy rings false, however. He may indeed care about Minosa's fate, but his intense interest—and by extension, the crowd's—is really a form of emotional self-indulgence. Surely, if he or a loved one were trapped he would hope for a rescue and public concern. But it is unlikely he would appreciate his struggle for survival becoming the centerpiece for a celebration. And yet he remains at the scene of the rescue and expresses indignation when another tourist claims to have been the first on the scene. In a radio interview, he even takes an opportunity to plug the insurance company he works for. His is a selfish form of compassion indeed.

RUBBERNECKERS

Like rubberneckers at real tragedies, Federber and his wife, Nellie, invoke a higher purpose to justify their curiosity. As he arrives on the scene and decides to stay, he says, "Wake up the kids, Nellie. They should see this. This is very instructive." The arrival of the Federbers—"To me, they're Mr. and Mrs. America," Tatum says—is a good omen for the success of the story. "I wasn't sure before," a relieved Tatum declares, "but now I know they're going for it."

Tatum's manipulation reaches to every facet of the story. Minosa's fear of imagined Indian spirits is exaggerated. The calculating sheriff is portrayed in news stories as "the tireless public servant who never spares himself." Tatum convinces Lorraine not to desert Minosa until the rescue is completed because public interest in the story is building, which will lead to land-rush sales at the restaurant she runs with Minosa. "They'll eat it up—the story and the hamburgers." Later, Tatum arranges a prayer service at a quaint chapel and assigns Cook to make sure Lorraine attends, instructing him to take rosary beads for her to hold in the photographs.

As the narrative unfolds, Cook finds himself slowly drawn into Tatum's world. As he watches Tatum operate, Cook, a recent journalism school graduate, realizes that his education has not fully prepared him to find and present news effectively. He comes to idolize Tatum, who becomes his guide and instructor. Tatum derides the idea of journalism education and chides Cook for his lack of news instincts. It is obvious that whatever journalistic shortcomings characterized the curriculum at Cook's college, there was also a complete absence of moral instruction.

The ethical models described in this chapter are not rigid templates. They are neither interchangeable nor mutually exclusive. An individual's own sense of right and wrong determines, to a large extent, his or her method of achieving virtue. That does not mean, however, that ethical models can be chosen instrumentally and employed to help a journalist find a solution that will justify the course of action that best suits his or her short-term needs.

Each of the models we've examined offers a different lens through which to view our roles and expectations and the potential consequences of our actions. Each model also helps us to draw a "moral map" by which we might navigate the ethical challenges journalists face daily. The point of ethics is not to pledge allegiance to one particular model or philosopher, but to survey the spectrum of ethical perspectives in order to form an honest view that helps us, as Bok urges, to honor public trust.

As Tatum's manipulations become increasingly bold and outrageous, Cook can only go along for the ride, raising half-hearted, almost inarticulate objections to his mentor's methods. Without a moral code in place, Cook's ideas of right and wrong shift with the wind. Without a grounding in ethical philosophy and a commitment to a clear vision of the public good, Cook cannot grasp the larger issues at stake in the ersatz drama of Minosa's rescue. Cook's education prior to his alliance with Tatum has covered only the most mundane and mechanical aspects of journalism, the rote processes by which facts are appraised, collected, and disseminated.

REDEMPTION

The rewards Tatum uses to tempt Cook are powerful—fame, wealth, and prestige. These are rewards that motivate many young people to pursue a particular career path, and they can be earned honestly. Tatum's road to reward is a shortcut. Just as he sees Minosa in a purely instrumental light, Tatum also sees the practice of journalism as instrumental to his own well being, instead of as a vital public trust.

Cook is entranced by the fact that his photographs are being circulated by the wire services and may garner him a spread in a popular magazine like *Life*. "There isn't anything you could do wrong as far as I'm concerned," he fawningly tells Tatum as the story reaches its climax.

Just as Tatum feels creeping guilt about Minosa's fate, he begins to question his role in Cook's corruption. Tatum initially defends himself against Booth's charge that he is teaching Cook "below the belt" journalism by dismissing Booth as bland and old-fashioned. Tatum also passes some of the blame for his methods to his audience. After slapping a smile off Lorraine's face and ordering her to look mournful, Tatum explains, "This is the way it reads best and this is the way it's going to be. It's the way people like it and it's the way I'm going to play it." When his conscience begins to gnaw at him, however, he blames the audience for demanding what he is selling.

When faced by intense criticism, the press often falls back on rationalizations, but, curiously, it also tends to lash out at the very audience that supports it. In the wake of an appalling episode of sensationalism, journalists often turn on the audience, publishing "think pieces" about the failings of the mass mind and explaining to higher-toned critics that they are simply providing the public with what it demands, as distasteful as it might be.

When Minosa dies, Tatum, too, takes a sanctimonious turn. Addressing the crowd from atop the "Mountain of the Seven Vultures," he admonishes the spectators to "go home . . . the circus is over." But who, after all, created the circus? The crowd at which Tatum sneers is there at his explicit invitation. The press cannot entirely evade responsibility for the level of discourse it provides by claiming "the public made us do it."

As a final act of redemption, after Minosa's death Tatum escorts Cook back to Booth's paper and sits him at a desk where he can write the honest story of the scheme that kept Minosa imprisoned and, ultimately, killed him. The story will destroy Sheriff Kretzer's reelection chances and likely spell the end of Smollett's contracting business. Tatum dies as his young protégé reclaims his place in Booth's virtuous newsroom. Cook has been returned to the light. There is hope for journalism after all.

Ace in the Hole might not be considered by aspiring journalists to be a rousing invitation to join the profession, but from its cynicism spring seeds of hope. The film bares the worst instincts of journalism on institutional, social, and personal levels, but points out that despite working within professional and social constraints, journalists have wide latitude to create and adopt—or ignore—ethical principles.

Tatum, as well as the editors who bid on his story from New York, choose to ignore their ethical duties. Booth, however, is not so easily tempted by the easy payoff of the Leo Minosa story because he has a thoughtful ethical philosophy and a conception of the public good in place. At the film's fadeout, Cook—and perhaps, by extension, every other young scribe with visions of Pulitzer Prizes and easy glory dancing in his or her head—is ready to begin a journey toward moral reasoning.

QUESTIONS TO CONSIDER

1. Is Tatum justified in taking over the rescue attempt and managing it while he is covering the event? In what ways do real reporters participate in the managing of the events they cover?

2. As the story explodes nationally, Tatum resigns from Booth's paper and offers his copy to the highest bidder in New York. Does Tatum owe Booth a debt of loyalty that should compel him to continue working for him until the story is resolved? In what circumstances might professional loyalty come into conflict with other loyalties?

3. Should reporters trade off their power to provide favorable publicity in return for the cooperation of public figures in gaining access to a story, as Tatum does by working hand-in-glove with the sheriff? In what ways might today's reporters make similar—if less outrageous—tradeoffs with the public figures they cover?

4. Is Tatum guilty of misrepresentation by not immediately informing Minosa that he is a reporter and by constantly

assuring Minosa he is acting primarily as Minosa's "pal" in orchestrating the rescue? Are reporters ever justified in concealing their identities and motives when pursuing a news story?

5. Does Tatum coach the emotional reactions of Minosa's family? Do news organizations ever "encourage" a particular emotional response, or ignore responses that don't fit with audience expectations?

6. Do the New York publishers and other reporters consider proportion and accuracy as they evaluate Tatum's dispatches? How well do your local newspapers and television stations meet standards of proportionality?

7. Is the crowd that is drawn to the dramatic rescue a victim of unethical newsmaking, or do its members share some complicity in the media circus that ensues? To what extent do readers and viewers today contribute to sensationalism?

8. Tatum acts not only as a newspaper reporter covering a story, but also as a spokesman for the rescue effort for the broadcast media. Do you think today's reporters sometimes make themselves the center of the stories they cover? Is that appropriate?

9. How does Cook's ethical code evolve as the story progresses? How can a reporter new to the profession go about constructing an appropriate and informed moral code?

10. Since it is Tatum's publicity that sparks a rescue attempt, are his actions, on the whole, justified? Would it be better if he had never stumbled on the scene? Would Leo have been better off if Tatum scrupulously observed his obligations to not interfere in the unfolding of a news story? Do you think news organizations wisely wield their power to draw attention to certain stories?

FURTHER READING

Christian, Clifford, Kim B. Rotzoll, and Mark Fackler. *Media Ethics: Cases and Moral Reasoning*. 4th ed. New York: Longman, 1995.

Hartley, Howard W. *Tragedy of Sand Cave*. Louisville, Ky.: Standard, 1925.

Klaidman, Stephen, and Tom Beauchamp. *The Virtuous Journalist*. New York: Oxford University Press, 1987.

Knowlton, Steven. *Moral Reasoning for Journalists*. Westport, Conn.: Praeger, 1997.

MacIntyre, Alasdir. *A Short History of Ethics*. New York: Simon and Schuster, 1996.

Manoff, Robert Karl, and Michael Schudson, ed. *Reading the News*. New York: Pantheon, 1986.

Meyer, Philip. *Ethical Journalism: A Guide for Students, Practitioners, and Consumers*. New York: Longman, 1987.

Murray, Robert, and Roger W. Brucker. *Trapped!: The Story of the Struggle to Rescue Floyd Collins from a Kentucky Cave in 1925*. New York: Putnam, 1979.

Patterson, Philip, and Lee Wilkins, eds. *Media Ethics: Issues and Cases*. 3rd ed. Boston: McGraw-Hill, 1998.

Rawls, John. *A Theory of Justice*. Cambridge, Mass.: Belknap, 1971.

2

Deadline U.S.A.:
The Wages of Virtue

Ed Hutcheson, managing editor of *The Day*, can be forgiven for snarling. The former wife for whom he still carries a torch is about to marry another man. Hutcheson's star reporter has been worked over by thugs—and their mobster boss is getting ready to lay some muscle on him. The advertising manager is making deals to keep unpleasant news about big spenders out of the paper's columns. And, to top it off, the dilettante daughters of *The Day*'s honorable founder are getting ready to sell the paper out from under him.

Against these overwhelming odds, Hutcheson, portrayed with weary integrity by Humphrey Bogart in 1952's *Deadline U.S.A.*, manages to navigate the last days of *The Day* with dignity and a sense of moral purpose. In a desperate but ultimately doomed effort to keep the paper alive, Hutcheson promises to show the public "how a real newspaper can function"—and he succeeds. As *The Day* comes to an end, Hutcheson and his staff race to expose a racketeer who is corrupting the unnamed city (clearly New York) where the movie is set.

Therein lies the paradox of *Deadline U.S.A.*, and the newspaper industry it depicts: editorial quality, reader loyalty, and community service have precious little to do with determining which news outlets survive and which die. The crusading and socially responsible

Day perishes not because it lacks quality, readers, or even profits. It is devoured by a shallow, sensational rival because *The Day*'s owners are more interested in short-term profit than in the public good or the democratic institution they hold in trust.

Deadline U.S.A. has been praised by film scholars for its realistic portrayal of how journalists really work. Following its release, a reviewer for the *New York Times* observed that it "laid out quite an authentic picture of a down-to-earth newspaper shop." The film also offers an insightful and biting exploration of the economic forces that have killed off nearly half of the nation's newspapers since the 1920s. Over the past five decades, bankruptcies, acquisitions, and mergers have led to an unparalleled concentration of ownership in the American media. In the newspaper business, the survivors have often compromised their civic duties in order to enrich stockholders and serve the political ends of corporate parents.

American newspapers were not sold, merged, and closed merely as a result of greed or avarice in the postwar years, however. American society was undergoing a rapid transformation, fueled by the swelling of suburbia and the popularity of the new medium of television. Newspapers no longer dominated public discourse. Nevertheless, they continued to offer communities a source of comprehensive news, information, and opinion; the compressed format of local television news cannot match newspapers for depth or detail.

Deadline U.S.A. provides a snapshot of this key historical moment in the development of American journalism, as well as a compelling vehicle by which to examine two dimensions of ethics. On one level, *Deadline U.S.A.* shows us how individuals can maintain ethical integrity while working within a vast organization whose policies and operations are, for the most part, beyond their personal control. On a larger level, the film explores how the owners of an organization dedicated to building both economic *and* civic capital can either ignore or honor their obligations to the community.

JOURNALIST, HEAL THYSELF

As the 1950s dawned, newspapers everywhere were dying. New York City, for instance, had dozens of mainstream newspapers in 1900. By 1950, that number had shrunk to six. Today, there are three. Elsewhere the situation is even bleaker. Smaller cities like Buffalo, Cleveland, and Baltimore are now one-newspaper towns. While many of these papers are of high quality, the fact that there is only one comprehensive news outlet available to citizens means that the marketplace of ideas has contracted. Fewer newspapers and fewer owners mean fewer perspectives in the nation's press. A newspaper with a monopoly has a captive audience. It can also be confident that if it operates below board, no rival will call it to account. At one time, chronicles of the misdeeds of rivals provided some of the liveliest stories in a paper's columns.

Even in the days of intense competition, ideological or economic prerequisites sometimes superseded a commitment to the public good at many papers and chains; the potential for such bias has grown worse as critical voices have faded. The size and power of media corporations troubled press critics as consolidation accelerated in the 1940s and 1950s because huge media outlets dominated the public forum, letting in perspectives they agreed with and ignoring or denouncing perspectives they disliked. Economic concentration seemed to be fostering an abuse of power and degradation of the marketplace of ideas that is at the center of our democracy.

In the late 1940s, for instance, *New York American* publisher William Randolph Hearst Jr., son of the notorious yellow journalist, aided the communist witch-hunt of Senator Joseph McCarthy, even though he knew McCarthy did not really have a list of communists in the U.S. State Department, as he had declared in several speeches. Many years later, after countless lives had been tarnished by black-listing and bogus charges, Hearst admitted that he not only sat on what would've been the scoop of the decade—that McCarthy had no list of communists—but also helped his political ally carry out a devastating deception.

"Joe gave us a call not too long after that speech (in which he claimed to have a list of 205 communists working for the U.S. State Department)," Hearst recalled in his autobiography. "And you know what? He didn't have a damned thing on that list. He said, 'My God, I'm in a jam . . . I shot my mouth off. So what am I gonna do now?' Well, I guess we fixed him up with a few good reporters."

In 1947, the Commission on the Freedom of the Press, composed chiefly of academics, issued an alarming report on the implications of a consolidated and biased cabal of news outlets for the future of democracy. The commission—led by scholar Robert M. Hutchins and popularly known as the Hutchins Commission—made several recommendations aimed at keeping the public dialogue diverse and open. The commission did not advocate government control of the press, but warned that such control might be inevitable if the press did not better police itself.

In his essay "The Social Responsibility Theory of the Press," Theodore Peterson observed that the Hutchins Commission report was the capstone of a half-century of press criticism. The commission's complaints read like a bill of particulars:

- The press served the business community over all others and allowed advertisers to shape editorial content and silence opposing views
- The press resisted social change
- The press's incessant focus on sensational stories crowded out coverage of significant and substantial events and degraded public morals
- The press invaded the privacy of individuals
- Publishers used the press's power to further their own political, economic, and ideological interests, often ignoring the greater public good in the process

As it tries to operate in the public interest and ensure its own survival, *The Day* will confront all of these trends. And while pressures from the outside threaten to kill *The Day*, internal temptations also make it difficult for the paper to maintain its high standards.

The reform-minded Hutchins Commission recommended that news organizations adopt a set of moral objectives to guide financial and newsgathering operations. The commission's recommendations were intended to promote openness, fair play, and inclusiveness in the nation's press. The commission urged newsgathering organizations to:

- Provide a truthful, comprehensive, and intelligent account of the day's events in a context that gives them meaning
- Provide a forum for the exchange of comment and criticism
- Project a representative picture of the constituent groups in society
- Present and clarify the goals and norms of society
- Ensure full access to the day's intelligence

Such standards could be met only if news organizations maintained safeguards to ensure editorial independence and protect news-gatherers from economic and ideological pressures as they pursued the truth. The Hutchins Commission's criticisms and recommendations provide a rich context to explore how political and commercial pressures threaten journalistic integrity and how a news organization can effectively serve its community by operating within a set of moral codes. *Deadline U.S.A.* went into production shortly after the release of the Hutchins report, and it is unlikely that the lead character is named Hutcheson by coincidence. The film is pretty nearly a dramatization of the commission's compelling but dry report.

Deadline U.S.A. has other real-life roots. Before moving on to Hollywood, writer-director Richard Brooks worked as a reporter at what was left of the famed *New York World*. There, Brooks watched the once-majestic newspaper decay as the heirs of its founder, the great journalist Joseph Pulitzer, squandered the patriarch's money and legacy. The *World*, universally considered the greatest newspaper in America at the time of Pulitzer's death in 1911, began a long decline under the management of his son. It was sold to the Scripps-Howard chain in 1931 and shortly thereafter was merged with the *New York Evening Telegram*. There are many allusions to the end of the *World* in *Deadline U.S.A.*; in one early scene, *Day* editor Frank Allen (Ed Begley) fondly recalls working with Pulitzer and his legendary editor Frank Cobb.

Deadline U.S.A. illustrates both the criticisms and recommendations outlined in the Hutchins report. It also highlights the economic forces that were undermining the democratic potential of the press and shows realistic characters grappling with ethical dilemmas on individual and organizational levels.

There is much more at stake in the struggle of *The Day* than the loss of jobs or the violation of abstract libertarian principles. As the deadline for the paper's closure looms, *The Day* conducts an all-out crusade to bring to justice mobster Tomas Rienzi. Official agencies have failed to stop Rienzi, largely because he has bribed the public officials elected to enforce the law. *The Day*'s pursuit of Rienzi illustrates how a free press can, through the power of exposure, right a civic wrong when state institutions fail in their duties. "A newspaper," Hutcheson asserts, "is published first, last and always in the public interest." By foregoing easy sensationalism, *The Day* shows how a newspaper can earn honest profits by serving that interest, though not enough profits to satisfy its greedy owners.

"LET TRUTH AND FALSEHOOD GRAPPLE"

"A free press, sir, like a free life, is always in danger," Hutcheson tells a potential investor who is squeamish about pouring his money into *The Day*. Indeed, a free press is the catalyst of a free society. Individuals in a democratic political system are considered to have natural rights to determine their own destinies and, through debate and the ballot, to determine the destiny of the state. The right to self-determination would be meaningless without the right to free expression. In *Areopagitica* (1633), John Milton provided the central metaphors of a free society. Such a society, Milton argued, must revolve around a "marketplace of ideas"—a public forum where all may speak, question, challenge, assent, and dissent. No voices should be stilled; when one individual is deprived of the right to express an opinion, the entire society suffers the loss of a perspective that might ultimately provide a path to the truth. In a pure marketplace of ideas, liars, schemers, fools, and heretics have as much right to speak as anyone else; today's heretic is often tomorrow's prophet. "Let truth and falsehood grapple," Milton wrote. "Whoever knew truth put to the worse in a fair fight?"

Before the advent of the mass media, the "marketplace of ideas" was in most respects a literal marketplace—a physical space where people gathered to debate their common affairs. In American politics, a last vestige of this democratic ideal exists in the New England town meeting. The first presidential primaries have traditionally been held in New Hampshire, a state with a small population and little national power relative to bigger neighbors, because the town meeting offers a symbolic stage to reenact our heritage.

In a populous, far-flung, transient, and mediated world, of course, members of a society can no longer conduct their affairs face to face. The market squares of big cities have virtually no political functions today; the new market square in most communities—the mall—is under the control of private owners who place strict limits on discourse. And so today our common forum is constituted in an abstract space by the media. Ideally, the news media should circulate information, air diverse ideas, and herald the proposal of new policies. To a great extent, they set the agenda for political, social, and moral debate.

Since ours is a capitalist as well as a democratic society, the news media, in addition to serving as the public's vehicles of democratic connection, are the private property of a relatively few firms and individuals. For instance, one company—Gannett—controls more than 10 percent of all American newspaper circulation (in addition to television stations and many other media ventures). In 1920, about 12 percent of newspapers were owned by chains; today, that figure is 90 percent. The trend is accelerating. In 2000, the Tribune Corporation acquired the Times-Mirror Corporation; as a result, Los Angeles's biggest daily newspaper is now operated by a Chicago-based conglomerate.

Navigating the tense division between profits and First Amendment responsibilities has never been easy. Control of the mediated marketplace of ideas offers extraordinary opportunities for economic gain, but it also carries responsibilities. For democracy to work, the public forum must be diverse and inclusive. Obviously, when the number of media outlets shrinks, and when those that remain come under the control of a few big corporations, the conditions under which democracy can thrive are threatened.

Hutcheson will argue this point to a surrogate court judge who is deciding whether to allow Margaret Garrison (Ethel Barrymore), the wife of the late John Garrison, to repurchase *The Day* after she regrets giving her consent to its sale. The right to property and capital underpin our economic system, Hutcheson acknowledges, but that right cannot be venerated to the exclusion of all other values. When a lawyer tries to silence Hutcheson because he is not legally a party to the transfer of the *Day*'s assets, Hutcheson points out that some assets are neither tangible nor convertible into dollars and cents.

"*The Day* consists of a big building—I don't own that," he says. "It also consists of typewriters, teletypes, press, newsprint, ink and desks—I don't own those either." *The Day*'s real asset is the First Amendment freedom it exercises in trust for the public. The employees and readers of *The Day* are stakeholders in the enterprise, whether they have stock certificates or not. "An honest, fearless press," Hutcheson thunders, "is the public's first protection from gangsterism, local or international."

Given the climate in which the film was released, it is unlikely the filmmakers wanted to antagonize the many newspaper chains that would review and advertise the film, and so Hutcheson makes a perfunctory nod to the quality of some newspaper chains. But his views on newspaper consolidation belie that sentiment; extensive chain ownership limits perspectives.

Echoing Milton, Hutcheson declares that "without competition there can be no freedom of the press . . . the right of the public to a marketplace of ideas, news, and opinions. Not of one man's, or one leader's, or even one government's." Private control of the press ensures that the government cannot monopolize the marketplace, but corporate monopoly is no better than government monopoly.

A decade after *Deadline U.S.A.* was released—and therefore decades before the modern merger mania—essayist Howard Luck Gossage asserted that

> it is too bad that so much is made of the constitutional guarantee of freedom of the press from government control, for it tends to obscure other incursions on freedom of the press that are just as dangerous and more immediate. That these incursions are economic rather than political makes them somehow more insidious and certainly much harder to recognize. So we are unlikely to look for incursions of our political freedoms in perfectly legitimate economic practices or to comprehend their enormous implications even when we find them staring us in the face.

At *The Day*, Hutcheson puts out a paper that reflects the spirit of the Hutchins report. A reporter eager to publish a seminude picture of murder victim Bessie Schmidt—who will play a key role in the paper's investigation of Rienzi—is rebuffed. Crime is dramatic and intriguing, but news organizations that highlight only the sensational aspects of crime, rather than its larger causes and effects, do the public no service. News organizations that provide little more than sensational crime coverage give citizens a distorted view of their society. Hutcheson sarcastically advises the editor to put the pictures "on postcards and send them to Paris. Play it down, second section. No pictures."

Similarly, as he discusses the play of a consequential story on a new tax policy, Hutcheson makes clear that his obligation is not to shovel bewildering facts at readers, but to help them interpret facts and put them in context. Confronted with a story full of bureaucratese on a tax hike, Hutcheson asks, "What does this tax program mean to the average man and woman? Not billions. That's an impossible figure. Break it down," he instructs his staff. "What will it cost a housewife for groceries? How much more for a new car? Or a radio? Fifty bucks? A hundred? How much?"

The Day's crusade against Rienzi is also constructed within a web of context. The mobster's activities are shocking and could be presented in a way that would merely outrage or titillate readers. But Hutcheson is after bigger game. He is using the paper, in the words of the Hutchins report, to "clarify the goals and norms of society." Rienzi does more than operate rackets; he fixes elections and bribes public officials. His activities degrade the entire community and rob citizens of their constitutional rights.

SCRIBES UNDER SEIGE

That *The Day* can operate at a level of journalistic and moral excellence is due to the guidance of one man—Ed Hutcheson. In fact, keeping *The Day* on the righteous path seems to require his constant presence; he can't even sneak away for dinner with his former wife without being called back to quell some crisis. If he doesn't shoulder the responsibilities, no one else will; his sense of commitment to *The Day* ruined his marriage in the first place.

Without Hutcheson, there would be no *Day*. The majority owners couldn't care less about the paper's content; the business department would be happy to design the paper to please advertisers; and the editorial employees, honorable and dedicated though they are, simply lack the power to run the show. Throughout the film, Hutcheson makes clear that his loyalties extend beyond his employers and employees. Ultimately, his loyalties are to the public.

His loyalty is not reciprocated. At the onset of the film, staffers who have dedicated themselves to making the paper great find out it is to be sold from an Associated Press (AP) dispatch. They can find no logic in the sale. "But we're the best outfit in town, in the country maybe. Why? Why sell?" an editor asks Hutcheson, who replies with resignation: "Money—that's usually the reason something is sold, isn't it?" In the luxurious dome atop *The Day* building, meanwhile, the plutocratic heirs of *Day* founder John Garrison do most of their talking through lawyers and treat their obligations to the people toiling below—both employees and readers—with flippancy and detachment.

Several levels of loyalty can be seen in *Deadline U.S.A.* Staff members of *The Day* must decide whether to remain loyal to each other even though the struggle they are engaged in is lost. On seeing the AP dispatch, one copy editor immediately places a call to another paper seeking a job. Later, a photographer refuses an assignment to photograph Rienzi, reasoning that risking his neck to get a picture for a paper about to fire him is absurd. Hutcheson hastens his departure from *The Day*. Even if the presses are to roll for only a few more days, he is going to see to it that the newspaper fulfills its obligations. Conversely, when an idealistic young investigative reporter trying to nail Rienzi is badly beaten, Hutcheson sends the man's wife money from his personal account and coerces a prominent specialist into postponing an international trip and performing an operation to save the reporter's eyesight.

The socialite daughters who have inherited *The Day* know little about their property, the role *The Day* plays in the community, or the people who depend on it for news and guidance. They feel no loyalty to their employees, their readers, or their father's legacy. When Hutcheson demands to know to whom the paper will be sold, daughter Alice Garrison responds, "What difference does it make?"

Hutcheson tries to no avail to explain to Garrison's daughters that because a newspaper plays a vital role in a democracy, it must be considered to be more than an accumulation of assets. Despite their promise to cut him in for 1 percent of the sale price, Hutcheson is disgusted by the prospect that the paper will be sold to sensational rival Lawrence White. White will shutter *The Day* as soon as possible to fatten the circulation and advertising of his paper, *The Standard*. "You're not selling *The Day*, you're killing it," Hutcheson declares. His exhortations help Margaret Garrison rediscover her own sense of loyalty to the paper and its readers.

"THOUGHTFUL DISPATCH"

Hutcheson laments the fact that while the late John Garrison was a great publisher, he was "a lousy father." The reason the heirs cannot see past the economic dimensions of their actions is that, unlike Hutcheson, no one, apparently, has given them moral instruction.

Maybe Garrison's daughters just weren't paying attention. The news business requires that reporters and editors act quickly and decisively, calculating the potential news value and moral consequences of stories in a split second. Throughout *Deadline U.S.A.*,

Hutcheson juggles several crises at once and rarely hesitates as he makes editorial and moral judgments.

Hutcheson can act with thoughtful dispatch because he has internalized a moral code he inherited from Garrison. As he argues with Garrison's daughters about the sale of *The Day*, he points to a framed copy of the first edition of *The Day* and recites its editorial principles; he has no need to read them because he knows them by heart. In the first edition of *The Day*, Garrison provided a civic and moral compass for the venture: "This paper will fight for progress and reform. It will never be satisfied merely with printing the news. It will never be afraid to attack wrong—whether by predatory wealth or predatory poverty." Later, even as the paper is dying, Hutcheson will write, under John Garrison's byline, a front-page editorial reiterating those principles.

If tangling with an angry mobster, cutthroat heirs, and an alienated former wife are not enough, Hutcheson also has to confront threats to *The Day* from within the newspaper. Large department stores provided much of the revenue during the heyday of urban newspapers and often expected more than advertising space for their money. In *Deadline U.S.A.*, department store magnate Wharton, *The Day*'s biggest advertiser, asks the paper's advertising manager to pull a story linking him to murder victim Bessie Schmidt. Afraid Wharton might withdraw his advertising dollars from *The Day*, the manager complies.

Legendary *Chicago Daily News* editor Melville Stone concisely summed up the inherent contradiction between truth-telling and profit-making. Stone directed his reporters to strive always for "accuracy and impartiality," but he acknowledged that a newspaper's financial interests ultimately shape its news columns. "In a certain sense," Stone said, "the counting room must have no influence in the matter, and yet in a longer sense it must have everything to do with it."

When Hutcheson discovers the bargain between Wharton and the advertising department, he has the integrity—and the authority—to confront the manager who ordered the story killed. "You're a big advertiser, Mr. Wharton," he tells the distraught store owner, "we need your business. But not on those terms." As the film makes painfully clear, however, Ed Hutcheson is a special kind of editor; such quid pro quo is commonplace at other papers.

On a more direct level, the press's dependence on and loyalty to advertisers can create conflicts between increasing profits and serving the public interest. Simply put, the public contributes far less—directly—to the bottom line of a news organization than do advertisers. "On the day a reader first bought a publication for less than it cost to produce," Gossage concluded, "he lost his economic significance and became circulation." The First Amendment, however, was not created primarily to enhance the profits of publishers. No economic paradigm should supersede the right of citizens to complete and truthful information.

A SCHOOL FOR SCANDAL

As he mourns *The Day* with loyal colleagues, Hutcheson expresses exasperation at how small a role real news plays in modern newspapers. "It's not enough anymore to give them just news—they want comics, contests, puzzles. They want to know how to bake a cake, win friends and influence the future, ergo horoscopes, tips on the horses, interpretation of dreams so they can win on the numbers lotteries. And—if they accidentally *stumble* on the first page—news."

In recent years, the morphing of news into "infotainment" has far exceeded what Hutcheson describes in *Deadline U.S.A.*, but the seeds of this trend are nearly as old as the American press. The need to entertain as well as inform is but another manifestation of the long standing tension between profit and service that has shaped journalism.

The progenitors of the inclusive Penny Press of the 1830s, Benjamin Day and James Gordon Bennett, pushed journalism beyond narrow boundaries of political information and commentary to give readers stories of crime, finance, high society, and human interest. Joseph Pulitzer further broadened the scope of newspapers by offering readers public opinion surveys, stunts—such as Nellie Bly's successful attempt to circumnavigate the globe in less than eighty days—and contests. Pulitzer was a serious social reformer, but he understood that reform ideas without an audience are impotent—and building an audience means catching the attention of readers. He explained his methods this way: "You may write the most sublime philosophy, but if nobody reads it where are you? You must go for your million circulation and once you have got it turn the minds and votes of your readers at critical moments."

Pulitzer also expanded the investigative ambitions of journalism. He probed corruption in government and business, and was not above sending reporters on undercover assignments to expose it. Pulitzer would understand perfectly why and how *The Day* sets out to nail mobster Rienzi.

The right of the press to be nosy has always clashed with the right to be left alone. In *Deadline U.S.A.*, Hutcheson's staff is able to pry into every facet of Rienzi's affairs—his finances, business connections, and even his sex life. In other instances in the film, Hutcheson opts to respect the privacy of news subjects as much as possible, but in the case of Rienzi, Hutcheson believes he is justified in aggressive snooping because exposure of the mobster's activities will serve the greater good by ending Rienzi's corruption.

But reporters and editors can also abuse the entrée to information they enjoy. *The Day* employs a professional researcher who can get the goods on anyone in record time. When Hutcheson squares off with his former wife's new boyfriend, he uses the resources of *The Day* to scour the man's past for any evidence of criminality or unseemly behavior. Alas, he finds none. But the mere fact that reporters can use their skills and access to public institutions to lay their hands on information about private individuals is unsettling. The information that Hutcheson gathers on his love rival is all part of the public record, but journalists have special training—and sometimes special access—in acquiring this information and must take care not to use it for selfish or personal ends.

A COURT OF LAST RESORT

Theoretically, the mass media are impersonal. By and large, the readers are unknown to the reporters and editors who bring them the news. But just as journalists have personal, organizational, and social loyalties, readers can also become devoted to a particular news organization or to individual reporters whose bylines they read and trust every day.

For engaged readers, the newspaper is more than a window on the world. It is a guide in public affairs, a schoolhouse, a court of last resort. Mrs. Schmidt, the mother of Rienzi's slain lover, ultimately begins the chain of events that allows Hutcheson and *The Day* to ensnare the racketeer. She takes her daughter's diary, which details Rienzi's many illicit enterprises, to Hutcheson because she trusts *The Day*.

At times, a bitter Hutcheson has had reason to question his ethical principles. After all, his devoted employees are being put out of work so an unscrupulous rival can acquire and close a newspaper he's given his heart and soul to. "Maybe if I'd given you this kind of newspaper, you'd still have jobs," he says at he glances at *The Standard*, which has plastered across its front page the photograph of Bessie Schmidt's seminude body—the same photograph Hutcheson had refused to print. But even though he ultimately loses the paper, Hutcheson's principles help him to accomplish his larger goal—the exposure of Rienzi and the advancement of the public welfare.

Hutcheson's temperate coverage of Bessie Schmidt's murder affirms her mother's loyalty to *The Day*, and by extension the loyalty of other readers who care about justice and decency. When Hutcheson asks Mrs. Schmidt why she is giving the diary to him instead of to the police, she replies in her broken Old Country dialect: "Police? I do not know the police. I know newspaper—this newspaper. For thirty-one years I know this newspaper. I come to America. I wish to be good citizen. How to do this? Newspaper. It shows me how to read and write. My Bessie dies. You do not say bad things about her. You do not show bad pictures of her. You try to find who hurt my Bessie. Good. I help."

Mrs. Schmidt remains adamant when Hutcheson warns her that cooperating with the paper could jeopardize her life; Rienzi, after all, has already murdered her daughter and son. "You are not afraid," she declares. "Your paper is not afraid. I am not afraid." The newspaper has served not only as an unofficial agent of justice in her daughter's death, but also as a model of civic virtue and courage.

When Rienzi warns Hutcheson that if *The Day* prints a story based on the diaries the editor will be "a dead man," Hutcheson scoffs. He is not attacking Rienzi on a personal basis. He is attacking the civic corruption that Rienzi represents. In *Areopagitica*, Milton acknowledged that falsehoods will sometimes prevail in the marketplace of ideas, but argued that ultimately a "self-righting principle" will cause the truth to prevail. Hutcheson invokes this principle and vows that *The Day* will be its agent. "People like you have tried it before with bullets, prisons, censorship—but as long as even one newspaper will print the truth, you're finished," he shouts over the din of the rolling presses. Sadly, that one newspaper vanishes from the community and the civic beacon that spells out *The Day* atop the building blinks out as the credits roll.

THE NEXT GENERATION

As he prepares to bury *The Day*, Hutcheson is approached by a young college student who has picked, it would seem, the absolute worst moment to ask for a job at the paper. Despite his pessimism about the future of journalism, an amused—and slightly drunk—Hutcheson takes a few moments to offer the kid some advice. He also tells him to stop by the office for a job, temporary as it will certainly be.

Hutcheson grins as the naïve young man tells of his ambition to start at the paper as a foreign correspondent to Egypt. Important assignments are earned, Hutcheson explains. They are made not as personal rewards, but because a news organization has decided that an individual possesses the expertise to fulfill an important public obligation. Sheepishly, the would-be Egyptian correspondent admits that aside from the fact that he can "speak a little French," he knows nothing of Egyptian politics, theology, or history.

Rather than ridicule the aspiring scribe, however, Hutcheson passes on the moral key to journalism that John Garrison handed down to him. "A newspaper man is the best profession in the world," he says, slurring slightly. "You know what a profession is?" When the kid answers that a profession is a skilled job, Hutcheson laughs. "Nope," he replies, "a profession is a performance for public good. That's why newspaper work is a profession."

As *Deadline U.S.A.* and the Hutchins report point out, news organizations can only meet a public-spirited definition of professionalism if they temper their right to pursue profits with an acknowledgment of their duty to honor the community interest and the fundamental democratic obligations of journalism.

"So you want to be a reporter?" Hutcheson asks before disappearing into the city's nightscape. "Here's some advice about this racket: Don't let 'em change your mind. It may not be the oldest profession, but it's the best."

QUESTIONS TO CONSIDER

1. How would you react if you were a reporter at *The Day* and were asked to carry out a potentially risky assignment knowing that the paper would soon close and leave you without a job? What loyalties might come into conflict and how would you resolve those conflicts?

2. *The Day*'s victory over Rienzi is a Pyrrhic one; in the end, the paper is sold and put out of business. Should the government have more power to regulate the operations and sale of news organizations? If you were asked to make a report to a government committee debating such regulation, what would you advise?

3. News and advertising departments at a news organization are, after all, part of the same company. Is it realistic to expect that newsrooms can be run free of interference from the business side of the organization? How might news organizations better manage the inevitable conflicts between the two? What's at stake if they do not?

4. While Hutcheson's larger motivations and objectives are just, he does engage in some ethically questionable practices. He sends a reporter to the home of the desperate brother of the victim to scare him into talking; unless he incriminates Rienzi, Herman Schmidt is warned, *The Day* will print his address so Rienzi can find and kill him. Hutcheson eventually pays Schmidt to tell his story. Are these tactics justified given Hutcheson's larger objectives in serving the public good?

FURTHER READING

Dillon, Mike. "William Randolph Hearst, Jr." In *American Newspaper Publishers: Dictionary of Literary Biography*, vol. 127, ed. Perry J. Ashley. Detroit, Mich.: Bruccoli Clark Lyman, 1993.

Gossage, Howard Luck. "Our Fictitious Freedom of the Press." In *Is There Any Hope for Advertising?* ed. Howard Luck Gossage, Kim Rotzoll, Jarlath Graham, and Barrows Mussey. Urbana: University of Illinois Press, 1986.

Hocking, William. *Freedom of the Press: A Framework of Principle.* Chicago: University of Chicago Press, 1947.

Laventhol, David. "The Life and Death of the Times Mirror." *Columbia Journalism Review* (May–June 2000).

Milton, John, *Areopagitica*. Christchurch: The Caxton Press, 1941.

Siebert, Fred S., Theodore Peterson, and Wilbur Shramm. *Four Theories of the Press*. Urbana: University of Illinois Press, 1963.

Stone, Melville. *Fifty Years a Journalist*. Garden City, N.Y.: Doubleday, Page, 1921.

Swanberg, W.A. *Pulitzer*. New York: Scribners, 1967.

3

All the President's Men: Truth and Consequences

Pity Alexander Leighton. In 1628, he published an essay arguing that the power of scripture trumped the power of England's King Charles I, who had instructed idealistic subjects with literary ambitions to follow a simple commandment: "Nothing shall be taught or maintained contrary to the King's instructions." The king's men took issue with Leighton's writings and he was hauled before the Star Chamber—a secret court—where his words were deemed "seditious and scandalous." His punishment served as a warning to other would-be contrarians: The authorities whipped Leighton, chopped off his ear, and slit one of his nostrils; once his face had begun to heal, they mutilated the other side. Leighton's deformity served as a walking reminder that ill-chosen words, like sticks and stones, can be quite painful.

John Twyn apparently didn't get the message. In 1663, he printed a sequel of sorts to Leighton's essay; this one aimed at Charles's sequel, his heir, Charles II. The son was as eager as the father to silence dissent and he outdid his namesake in meting out retribution. Twyn was arrested and tried; when he refused to finger the author of the pamphlet—an early example of a scribe shielding his sources—the king's men took care of him, too. His "privy members" were cut off as he watched. After he was disemboweled, his head was chopped off and his body quartered; pieces of his corpse were nailed to different gates that led into London.

Leighton and Twyn fought the law and the law won.

Three hundred and nine years after Twyn's gruesome end, two brash young newspaper reporters on the margins of their profession published worse things about their country's leader than Twyn ever had about his, and they became heroes and millionaires for their trouble. President Richard M. Nixon, threatened by exposure of the corruption and political espionage that came to be known as "Watergate," had at his disposal unlimited funds, fanatical flunkies, the Federal Bureau of Investigation (FBI), and the Central Intelligence Agency (CIA). No matter. In the end, his fall from grace was set in motion by two young journalists armed with notebooks. The episodes are not unrelated. To a great extent, Leighton and Twyn—and many other ink-stained reformers, revolutionaries, prophets, and madmen—made the world safe for Bob Woodward and Carl Bernstein.

All the President's Men, based on the best-selling book about the Watergate investigation by Woodward and Bernstein and directed by Alan J. Pakula, was released in 1976—the nation's bicentennial—and depicted events whose ramifications were (and are) still being felt in American society. The film chronicles the efforts of the *Washington Post* to unravel a presidential conspiracy that surfaced with a bungled burglary attempt of the Democratic National Headquarters in the Watergate Hotel and Office complex.

The plot of the film (whose title alludes to both the nursery rhyme and the classic political novel *All the King's Men* by Robert Penn Warren) is as old as yarns about journalism: Two young, untested reporters uncover the story of their lives and then must fight both the power of the state and skeptics at their own newspaper to bring the facts to light. Dogged reporting and a never-say-die attitude carry them over every obstacle in their path, and, in the end, despite some dark moments, they get their man and the Republic is saved. Their tale, however, is rooted in the real-life events of America's most notorious political scandal (so far).

Film is, of course, an intimate medium and *All the President's Men* compresses the *Washington Post*'s courageous and complicated exposure of Watergate into the personas of two extremely telegenic reporters portrayed by Robert Redford and Dustin Hoffman. Although it is based on the real events of the Watergate scandal, in cinematic terms *All the President's Men* is a buddy movie, much like

Butch Cassidy and the Sundance Kid, a western about two charming outlaws that propelled Redford to stardom a few years earlier. Only this time Butch and Sundance wear the white hats and lead the posse that relentlessly chases the Constitution-rustling bad guys to the ends of the earth and back.

That said, *All the President's Men* goes beyond Hollywood clichés to offer glimpses into the larger relationships among reporters, news organizations, the state, and the public, and serves as a case study of the balancing act that is constitutional democracy. The film also provides a tableau of ethical decision making at individual and institutional levels. Woodward and Bernstein demonstrate a strong sense of duty and a consuming tenacity in pursuing the story, but their interactions with their sources also raise troubling questions about privacy, coercion, and deception.

FAIL-SAFE

America's founders knew well that when power is concentrated in one institution, tyranny follows. The Revolutionary War was fought not because the colonists hated the British—after all, most *were* British—but because the British system of government offered them no avenue for representation and the "redress of grievances."

In designing a new state, the founders looked into their own natures and experiences and concluded that when one man or institution is invested with absolute authority, abuse will surely follow. For that reason, the American state is divided into three branches of government. The president cannot pass laws; only Congress can. If Congress passes a law contrary to the interests of the people or the Constitution, the president can veto it, or the Supreme Court can strike it down. A government composed of institutions with competing mandates and responsibilities will by nature be constantly at odds with itself. American democracy is not the most efficient system, but it is designed to prevent one single institution from monopolizing power and authority. Even an unresolved presidential election cannot prevent the nation from going about its business.

The press has been described as the Fourth Estate. If the three branches of the state fall out of balance, if the system of checks and balances between institutions breaks down, the press—which theoretically speaks to and for citizens—can restore balance by exposing government malfeasance. The notion of checks and balances is consistent with the Newtonian worldview described in chapter 6 concerning the film *12 Angry Men*.

The power of this Fourth Estate has grown in the twentieth century. Early publishers who challenged the state were punished by means of libel laws, taxes, and tariffs. Because publishers were typically individuals who earned their bread by operating a press, they did not have the resources to stand up to the state. Today's press is politically and financially powerful. It has the means to fight incursions on its rights.

A free press in theory is easy to exalt; a free press in fact is something altogether different, especially to those who hold power. Thomas Jefferson's declaration that "Were it left to me to decide whether we should have a government without newspapers, or newspapers without a government, I should not hesitate a moment to prefer the latter," is conveniently remembered by journalists and their defenders. They understandably are not anxious to dwell on Jefferson's revised opinion, the one he formulated after colonial gadfly Thomas Callendar printed stories charging the third president had fathered children with his slave-lover (stories Jefferson swore were untrue): "Nothing can now be believed which is seen in a newspaper. Truth itself becomes suspicious by being put into that polluted vehicle."

All the President's Men portrays journalists operating at the zenith of their civic responsibilities; when the institutions empowered to check the illicit exercise of power failed to do so, the *Washington Post* and other news organizations stepped in. But the ethical dilemmas the *Post* and its reporters faced along the way beg the question of whether it is sometimes necessary to be dishonest in order to expose a larger truth—in this case, a story crucial to the future of American democracy.

MEANS AND ENDS

Had the Watergate stories failed to link President Nixon to political corruption, the events depicted in *All the President's Men* might have provided the raw material for a very different kind of narrative about the press. It is easy to imagine a scarred Nixon aide writing a memoir about an irresponsible press hungry to trigger a constitutional crisis and reporters and editors apathetic to the rights and feelings of individuals they deemed useful to their story. Lost in the glow of adulation for Woodward and Bernstein is the fact that in the course of pursuing the Watergate story, they lied, used information from anonymous sources whose motives could not be discerned by readers, betrayed at least one source to whom they had promised confidentiality, violated the civil liberties of other citizens, interfered with the judicial process, and deceived or coerced sources who wanted to remain silent.

In the end, their work accomplished a larger good: President Nixon, who was illegally using the power of the federal government to discredit and disable potential political rivals—a dire violation of the Constitution in fact and spirit—was exposed and driven from office. A key ethical question, however, remains: Does the fact that the *Washington Post* was instrumental in bringing Nixon and his henchmen to justice excuse any unethical acts that were necessary to achieve that justice? A central question of ethics since Greek times has been: Do the ends justify the means? Is an unethical act justified if it helps to achieve a broader "ethical" objective?

For instance, early in the film, a stymied Bernstein, trying to link various actors in the nascent conspiracy, implores a reluctant source at the phone company to provide him with several individuals' phone records, which the phone company is forbidden by law to disclose. Bernstein's source points out the irony of violating the civil rights of individuals in order to expose government's violation of civil rights. "Carl, if John Mitchell was after your phone records, you'd be screaming invasion of privacy," the source observes.

The ethical conflict between means and ends that underlies *All the President's Men* is one reporters must negotiate on a daily basis. For instance, in 1993 ABC News reporters decided to conceal their identities (and their cameras) for an exposé on a supermarket selling tainted meat. The reporters got the story they were after, but to accomplish their ends they had to fill out deceptive job applications and betray the trust of coworkers at the store, who were unaware they were on camera. And, in 1998, *Cincinnati Enquirer* reporter Michael Gallagher decided that exposing alleged illegal business practices by Chiquita Brands International, the banana company, justified illegally obtaining company voice mail messages. Within a month of publication, the *Enquirer* was forced to renounce the series and Gallagher was fired. In addition to printing a front-page apology, the *Enquirer* paid Chiquita $10 million in damages.

Most reporters would agree that truth-telling is a central function of journalism, but these cases—and some of the practices illustrated in *All the President's Men*—seem to indicate that truth-telling is paramount only in the news report itself, not in the practices that produce it. Even the formal codes of ethics formulated by journalists are ambivalent about what methods journalists can use without crossing ethical boundaries. For instance, the Society of Professional Journalists (SPJ) instructs members to identify sources "whenever feasible." It discourages the use of undercover methods except as a last resort and admonishes reporters to respect the integrity and privacy of individuals.

Journalists argue that in some cases deception is the only way to get important news stories. Bad guys rarely give up the goods on themselves on the record, but they may make unguarded statements or take illegal actions when they are convinced they are operating in privacy. While tricking a trickster might be an effective course of action, making a decision to deceive based on the relative moral status of the deceived—fighting fire with fire—is not defensible ethically. Such a rationale is too easily bent to suit an actor's purposes.

What makes the deceptions of *All the President's Men* fascinating is that the two well-meaning reporters sometimes use deception to trick morally upright people into telling what they know about wrongdoers. This is morally ambiguous territory indeed. But the actions of Woodward and Bernstein are not necessarily beyond the pale. Many ethicists agree that deception may be justified under some compelling circumstances.

The Poynter Institute for Media Studies, for example, has concluded that deception is morally permissible if, among other things, the information reporters stand to gain is "profoundly important," all other alternatives to get it have been exhausted, and the journalists deliberated carefully before acting. Poynter guidelines also require reporters to eventually disclose any deceptive practices they used to get the story.

Ethical decision making does not happen by accident. The First Amendment is in itself a declaration of ethics; the right to speak and write freely helps to ensure the integrity and autonomy of the individual. But it does not follow that an action protected by the First Amendment is necessarily ethical. Ethicist Deni Elliott points out that "comments such as . . . 'the First Amendment means that no one can tell us what to do' tend to divert journalists' and consumers' attention from careful consideration of important ethical issues."

Elliott argues that journalists should never employ deceptive practices lightly or without considering whether their actions would cause or prevent a larger moral transgression. Echoing the Poynter guidelines, Elliott argues that journalists should not engage in practices they do not believe they can defend in good conscience publicly. By these standards, many of the tactics the *Post* used to pursue the Watergate story—such as pressuring and deceiving sources, granting anonymity, and running information whose accuracy could not be definitively verified—seem to be on shaky ground while others appear to be defensible. By examining some particular episodes that raise ethical questions, we can begin to fashion a rational and moral framework for the actions of the *Washington Post* in *All the President's Men*.

MAY I COME IN?

Sandra L. Borden and Michael Pritchard point out that reporters deceive sources for some very good practical reasons: Sources are more likely to speak candidly if they believe they won't be quoted. In addition, reporters often reason that the "public's right to know" outweighs the desire of individual sources to preserve their privacy.

In *All the President's Men*, Carl Bernstein is charming and impetuous. His faux pas are played for comic relief, but his actions raise serious questions about the methods reporters use to gather information that sources are reluctant to give. When a reporter conceals or misrepresents his identity or purpose, a source is deprived of information needed to decide if it is in his or her best interests to speak out. We say many things in our homes or among friends we would not want conveyed to an audience of thousands, or even millions.

Bernstein's aggressive pursuit of the truth is admirable, but some of his tactics are ethically debatable—such as when he talks his way into the house of a reluctant CREEP bookkeeper (CREEP was the apt acronym of the Committee to Reelect the President) and takes advantage of her courteousness to coax out of her a story she clearly does not want to tell. The bookkeeper is not a public figure and has little experience dealing with reporters. Bernstein does all he can to disguise the fact that he will use the information she reveals to write a story. Taking out a notebook, he tells the bookkeeper, "Don't pay any attention to this, this is for my memory. I have a bad memory." Meeting up with Woodward later, he gleefully recounts how he covertly filled in his notes during numerous trips to the bathroom. Bernstein reveals he is also driven by a desire to get the story before another news outlet does.

Bernstein: Boy, that woman was paranoid! At one point I . . . I suddenly wondered how high up this thing goes, and her paranoia finally got to me, and I thought what we had was so hot that any minute CBS or NBC were going to come in through the windows and take the story away.

Woodward: You're both paranoid. She's afraid of John Mitchell and you're afraid of Walter Cronkite.

Later, the reporters scheme to squeeze more information out of the reluctant bookkeeper by deceiving her. Thanks to Bernstein's penchant for unusual confirmations, the reporters know that the last name of one of the conspirators begins with letter "P," but two men under suspicion have names that fit. The reporters believe "P" refers to Bart Porter, but they must make sure before naming him in a story. This time, Woodward leads the duo down the path to deception as he proposes they trick her into confirming Porter's identity:

Woodward: We go back there and you ask her who "P" is, and then I say, no, we know "P" is Porter.

Bernstein: You mean we fake her out?

Woodward: Right.

Bernstein: And what if she denies it?

Woodward: We're screwed. But if she doesn't, we know we've got it.

The scheme works as planned, but journalists should remember that news sources and subjects are not cut-out characters to be manipulated in news stories. They are people, many of whom are thrust into public view for the first time because of a news story. Reporters who treat news subjects instrumentally—merely as fodder for a "great story"—fail to exercise empathy and to acknowledge that their own fallibility could easily turn them into subjects of a news story. Journalists must constantly ask themselves, "How would I want to be treated if I were the subject of this story?"

Ethical obligations extend beyond sources. A person who tempts or coerces someone else into acting unethically bears a share of moral responsibility. It is Bernstein who pressures a *Post* colleague to use her former boyfriend to obtain a list of CREEP employees. Woodward, at first, agrees with the strategy, but withdraws the request when he realizes how offensive their suggestion has been. Bernstein chastises his partner for his display of empathy, but eventually the bitter colleague produces the list.

Woodward and Bernstein pressure another *Post* colleague, Sally Aiken, into revealing a rendezvous with a married White House aide who boasted to her that he wrote a letter purporting to show that Democratic presidential hopeful Edwin Muskie had made an ethnic slur. She agrees to help, but is taken aback by the reporters' callousness.

> *Woodward*: Do you think he said it to impress you, to try to get you to go to bed with him?
>
> *Bernstein*: Jesus!
>
> *Woodward*: No, I want to hear her say it. Do you think he said that to impress you, to try to get you to go to bed with him?
>
> *Bernstein*: Why did it take you two weeks to tell us this, Sally?
>
> *Aiken*: I guess I don't have the taste for the jugular you guys have.

Bernstein, especially, seems willing to sacrifice personal honesty to the larger goal of obtaining accurate information. For instance, when he cannot get in to interview a Florida district attorney, Martin Dardis, he lures Dardis's secretary away from her desk by impersonating a court official on the telephone and directing her to retrieve documents at another office.

At the same time, Woodward and Bernstein are indignant when sources deceive *them*. Bernstein justifies tricking the secretary by reasoning that he has wasted an entire day flying to Florida and waiting in Dardis's office. But when an FBI source recants a confirmation, Woodward and Bernstein threaten to betray him and tell his boss he has been the source of leaks (this episode is detailed in the book, but glossed over in the movie). While both reporters routinely give cryptic answers to sources who want to know what they are driving at, Woodward explodes in anger at Deep Throat for not telling all he knows he about the Watergate conspiracy. On the other hand, both reporters acknowledge that sources who give them information do so at great risk. Neither expects, nor wants, innocent players in the Watergate drama to sacrifice their livelihoods to help them crack the story. They freely offer anonymity (a practice that will be explored presently) and acknowledge that what they are asking of their sources is not easy.

Most of the sources who are manipulated or misled by Woodward and Bernstein in *All the President's Men* are either puckered functionaries (Dardis's secretary) or wicked henchmen (fatuous dirty-tricks specialist Donald Segretti) and seemingly deserving of the reporters' relatively minor deceits. But reflexively taking the position that deception is acceptable if the person you are deceiving is dishonest, or that unethical acts are appropriate when they serve a greater ethical purpose, can lead one down a dangerous path.

"I'LL NEVER QUOTE YOU"

The Watergate conspiracy was ultimately exposed, but the mystery surrounding a key figure in the saga has only intensified in the quarter-century following Nixon's resignation: Who was Deep Throat?

Bob Woodward has vowed that he will not disclose his key source's identity until Deep Throat draws his last breath. Portrayed by Hal Holbrook, Deep Throat is a weary, vaguely sinister figure partial to midnight meetings in parking garages. His anonymity has lent greatly to Woodward and Bernstein's fame: Had he simply stood up and blown the whistle on the illegal doings in the White House—he apparently had the knowledge, credibility, and authority to do so—he, not the fearless reporters, would have been forever associated with Watergate.

While Deep Throat was reluctant to provide information directly to Woodward, he steered him to fruitful avenues of inquiry and confirmed facts the reporters had excavated from lesser sources. To know what he knew, Deep Throat had to have been a very powerful governmental figure, perhaps even a White House insider. The clues he provided were borne out by the reporters' own efforts and subsequent federal investigations. But while his role in the Watergate scandal helped to accomplish a civic good, his motives raise questions about the extent to which powerful figures should be allowed to manipulate the press to achieve their own personal or political objectives.

A source who is granted anonymity does not have to face the consequences of his or her words. Government officials often seek anonymity so they can float policy ideas in public without having to answer for them if the reception is negative. They also sometimes leak information anonymously to scuttle the initiatives, or even the careers, of political rivals.

Whistle-blowers who might lose their jobs if they are identified as the sources of sensitive information in a news story—for instance, a minor police functionary who leaks information about a brutality case that has been covered up—may well deserve the cloak of anonymity. But powerful public officials who have sought and accepted jobs that require public accountability should not be given anonymous access to the news columns to accomplish personal political objectives or to avoid accountability.

A REASON TO DECEIVE

Like the Poynter Institute and the SPJ, ethicist Edmund B. Lambeth begins his analysis of deceptive tactics with a declaration that any information acquired by deceptive means must be important. Lambeth, however, draws on deeper philosophical currents to explain his qualified support for deceptive practices. In his view, all of the following criteria must be met before a deceptive act can be undertaken:

1. The wrongdoing to be exposed should be wide-ranging and systemic. Using deceptive tactics to ensnare a single politician in a rendezvous with a prostitute would not be justified. But if the acts of one or several politicians were corrupting the very essence of the system they were elected to serve, deception might be warranted. By this criteria, many of Woodward and Bernstein's deceptive tactics seem to be ethically defensible because the Nixon White House was conducting a massive criminal enterprise whose tentacles spread into almost every facet of government. As Deep Throat points out, the conspiracy "involves the entire U.S. intelligence community. The FBI, the CIA. Justice. It's incredible."

2. The wrongdoing that would be exposed by deceptive acts will not be corrected if journalists fail to act. If a reporter tricks a grand juror into disclosing a grand jury verdict one day before it is to be announced, thereby scooping the competition, this condition would not be met and the deception would be unethical because it serves only the reporter's ends and undermines the integrity of a vital civic institution. Lambeth's second criteria is apparently met by much of the *Post*'s coverage of Watergate because the agencies that should have been investigating Nixon's activities did not fulfill their duty to do so.

Woodward and Bernstein did not bring Nixon down by themselves. As the story gathered steam, other newspapers and newsmagazines broke important stories about corruption in the White House. But it was not simply bad publicity that forced Nixon to resign. Instead, the press's incessant exposure of White House crimes served as a catalyst to government institutions to fulfill their duties to investigate and adjudicate. The *Washington Post* led the charge. In a *Post*-sponsored Internet interview twenty-five years after the scandal, Ben Bradlee observed that "we probably do get too much credit for it. There were many courageous people in government and in the press who deserve a lot of credit. But for the first seven months after the Watergate break-in, the *Post* was alone most of the time, keeping this story on the national agenda."

3. Deception may be justified if the wrongdoing it will help to expose "strikes at the heart of the social contract" and violates a fundamental social value such as justice or freedom. In hindsight, the Watergate story meets this test because Nixon's illegal actions were a direct threat to the nation's social compact, the Constitution. As the film moves to its dénouement, Bradlee (Jason Robards) exhorts his reporters to keep pressing because, despite public apathy and skepticism by other news outlets, the story's ramifications are huge:

> You know the results of the latest Gallup Poll? Half the country never even heard of the word Watergate. Nobody gives a shit. You guys are probably pretty tired, right? Well, you should be. Go on home, get a nice hot bath. Rest up . . . 15 minutes. Then get your asses back in gear. We're under a lot of pressure, you know, and you put us there. Nothing's riding on this except the, uh, First Amendment to the Constitution, freedom of the press, and maybe the future of the country. Not that any of that matters, but if you guys fuck up again, I'm gonna get mad. Goodnight.

By many of the criteria we've examined, it appears that Woodward and Bernstein were on solid ethical ground in deciding to deceive. But appearances, too, can deceive. There is a problem here. While ethical transgressions later in the investigation might be justified by the threat to social well-being posed by the Watergate conspirators, it does not absolve those that occurred earlier. The *Post* did not fully understand the magnitude of the events set into motion by the Watergate burglary until quite late in the investigation.

As he puzzles over the future direction of the reporting, Bradlee admits in the filem that the point of the story is not clear. "Look," he says. "McGovern's dropped to nothing, Nixon's guaranteed the renomination, the *Post* is stuck with a story no one else wants, it'll sink the goddamn paper. Everyone says, 'Get off it, Ben,' and I come on very sage and I say, uh, 'Well, you'll see, you wait till this bottoms out.' But the truth is, I can't figure out WHAT we've got." And so when Bernstein illegally obtained phone records he had no idea the story would become as wide-ranging and consequential as it did. Similarly, Woodward could not have imagined the scope of the conspiracy when he first granted carte blanche anonymity to Deep Throat.

Looking back, it is easy to say that since Watergate *did* threaten the nation, since Nixon *was* using the power of his office to sabotage political opponents, and since Woodward and Bernstein *were* able to unravel the conspiracy, any harm they may have done by deceiving individuals or readers is outweighed by the harm they prevented to society at large. But ethics doesn't work that way. The conditions that might allow us to act in a way that under ordinary circumstances would be considered unethical must be present *when we act*. It may be true that "everything worked out for the best" in the Watergate investigation, but that does not absolve the *Post* or its reporters of ethical responsibility for actions they took before the high stakes of the story were apparent.

Does that mean that the Woodward, Bernstein, and the *Post* should not have proceeded with their investigation? Not necessarily. One of the key requirements of every ethical model is deliberation. An impulsive action may indeed produce a beneficial outcome, but it cannot truly be said to be ethical. Ethics springs from moral reasoning. Even though they might have erred at times, the reporters and editors of the *Washington Post* did consider the ethical ramifications of their decisions and did deliberate before they acted. They did their best to think through the consequences their actions might trigger. Media credibility suffers immeasurably when media organizations cross ethical lines for no compelling reason or when media workers make it clear they gave little or no thought before taking actions that harmed subjects and outraged audiences.

Reporters who use deceptive tactics to batter lesser miscreants and then shrug at charges of unfairness do themselves and their profession no honor. ABC News, for instance, could have gotten its tainted meat story without deceiving Food Lion, but only at the expense of sacrificing ratings-friendly narrative tension and dramatic, grainy photography.

Despite ethical lapses during their investigation of Watergate, the journalists of *All the President's Men* also honor ethical ideals— namely their obligations to tell the story truthfully and to give their full effort to its pursuit.

PSYCHIC ARITHMETIC: ACCURACY

The Watergate stories had far-reaching consequences and illustrate the difficulty in pinning down the truth in a complex investigation. The journalists of *All the President's Men* take pains to publish accurate stories and avoid the temptation to present those stories within a frame of breathless sensationalism. As evidence points to an ever-widening conspiracy, the *Post* reacts with skepticism and alarm, rather than glee. Even Harry Rosenfeld (Jack Warden), who champions the two young reporters, recoils as the story gets closer to the Oval Office. "I happen to love this country," he says. "You know, we're not a bunch of zanies trying to bring it down."

Journalists should make sure the information they print is accurate and framed within a comprehensible context. Unless the connections between discrete facts are explained, stories are of little value to reader-citizens. The journalists of *All the President's Men* are zealous in their quest to publish accurate stories, but their deliberations as they prepare those stories vividly point out the temptations to go beyond the facts for the sake of a more powerful story.

Seemingly inseparable, Woodward and Bernstein come to be known in the *Washington Post* newsroom as "Woodstein." The moniker is apt because the two reporters seem to comprise a single personality. Both are driven, ambitious, and committed to the Watergate story, but each has his own style and standards.

Both reporters are concerned with accuracy. The *Post*'s Watergate investigation unfolded over a two-year period and consisted of hundreds of individual stories. Inaccurate stories would not only have been irresponsible, they would have wrecked the credibility of the *Post* and derailed the investigation. In *All the President's Men*, each reporter uses different criteria to decide if a potential story is accurate enough to merit publication.

Bernstein, like the old-style Hollywood reporter, relies on hunches. He believes a kind of psychic arithmetic can be used to draw conclusions from fragmented facts. Woodward, on the other hand, is methodical and rational. While Bernstein takes notes on matchbooks and scraps of paper, creates elaborate systems to confirm facts, and takes the expedient, but uncertain, step of having some sources identify Watergate conspirators by their initials instead of by their names, Woodward keeps careful records and types up his notes after interviewers. Woodward functions as Bernstein's rational conscience, a Jiminy Cricket who brings his partner back to Earth by challenging his insightful, but often unprovable, conclusions, conclusions that are based on a combination of intuition and observation. Bernstein becomes exasperated when Woodward rejects his argument that circumstantial evidence and his "gut feeling" provide an adequate basis for a story declaring there was a White House cover-up. A rather fanciful dialogue that mixes the Socratic and the sophomoric serves to contrast each reporter's attitude toward facts and the conclusions that might be drawn from them:

Bernstein: Well then, I don't know what you need. So you tell me what you need.

Woodward: I need more facts for a story. I think you should need the same.

Bernstein: If you get in a car and there's music playing in the car, hypothetically, and there is music playing in the car for ten minutes and there's no commercials, what can you deduce from that? Is it AM or FM?

Woodward: Okay, a guy comes up to me on a street and he asks me for an address. Is he interrogating me or is he lost? What kind of story do I write? What kind of deduction do I make from that?

Post editor Ben Bradlee, who must deal directly with the dangers the stories pose to the newspaper, constantly tests his reporters, questioning their facts, conclusions, and choice of sources. The reporters' task is to get the facts and produce stories; the editor's duty is to consider the larger ramifications of those stories. Editors decide if, how, and where stories should run. When Woodward and Bernstein prepare to write a story naming presidential aide Bob Haldeman as a conspirator in the scheme to use a gigantic and illegal slush fund controlled by CREEP to pay off Nixon's political saboteurs, Bradlee is skeptical. "We're about to accuse Haldeman, who only happens to be the second most important man in this country, of conducting a criminal conspiracy," he thunders. "It would be nice if we got it right."

The *Post*, however, does not get it right. In an effort to get additional confirmation for the story, Bernstein strikes an unusual agreement with a reluctant source. Bernstein will stay on the phone and if the man doesn't hang up by the count of ten, Bernstein can assume the story is correct. In his memoirs, Bradlee called the scheme "a gimmick that plowed new—and unholy—ground in the annals of journalism." The source misunderstands the complicated instructions and the *Post* runs a story true in substance, but inaccurate in its details.

The story hinges on whether CREEP aide Hugh W. Sloan Jr. implicated Haldeman in the secret fund to the grand jury investigating Watergate. Sloan had indicated to Woodward and Bernstein that Haldeman had controlled the fund. The reporters assumed Sloan must have given this information in his testimony to the grand jury. Haldeman did, in fact, control the fund, but Sloan did not testify to the fact because the grand jury never asked him—another indication that working behind a veil of secrecy, the government agencies charged with getting to the bottom of Watergate were trying their best not to.

WHO *ARE* THOSE GUYS?

As it is couched in the Bill of Rights, the First Amendment is a "negative" right. The central notion that all have the right to speak is merely implicit in the amendment's admonition that "Congress shall make no law" that impinges on an individual's right speak freely. We are only free *to* speak because we are free *from* government oppression. Ethics might seem to have a similar negative nature; that is, ethical behavior occurs because we refrain from taking certain actions, such as deceiving sources, granting anonymity, and publishing sensational allegations.

Ethical behavior, however, also requires positive action. Reporters cannot fulfill their civic obligations without specific goals and standards. Most ethicists agree that in addition to using ethics as a brake on potentially harmful actions, reporters and editors should strive mightily to discover and publish accurate information of consequence to citizens. A reporter who scrupulously avoids deceiving sources or

readers, but lazily reprints handouts from official sources is not ethical. An ethical reporter must also be tenacious in pursuing stories.

To say that Woodward and Bernstein are tenacious would be a co-
lossal understatement. If one journalistic standard characterizes the
duo, it is the tenacity that enables them to beat their competition to
the punch on almost every big Watergate development.

"Facts" pour into a news organization by the bushel basket, and
a lazy reporter can easily weave endless trite stories from them. A
tenacious reporter, however, is a seeker of truth, not a collector of
facts. In order to meet the ethical standard of tenacity, a journalist
must give maximum effort to pursuing stories that affect the public
interest.

The simple—and largely accurate—explanation of how two obscure reporters beat out their prominent peers to expose the biggest
political story of the twentieth century is that Woodward and
Bernstein thought and operated like eager cop reporters instead of
political reporters. Shut out of the closed loop of Washington
politics—the "Beltway"—they had no choice but to build their story
from the ground up, prying loose tidbits of information from relatively minor players in the White House and CREEP. Woodward's
naiveté about Washington politics is so great that at the outset of the
story he does not recognize the names of the high officials in his notebook. When he asks Rosenfeld who presidential aide Chuck Colson
is, Rosenfeld replies: "You know, I'm glad you asked me that. Because if you asked [*Post* editors] Simon or Bradlee that, they'd say,
'You know, we're going to have to fire this schmuck at once because
he's so dumb.'"

Washington politics and journalism operate within a symbiotic relationship that plays out in a cozy and privileged world, where government officials and reporters routinely exchange their respective
favors—information and publicity—over leisurely lunches at posh
restaurants. Such a convivial arrangement is adequate to the task of
conveying the routine business of government. But official sources
cannot be expected to provide reporters with information that would
lead to their own undoing. Operating outside of this incestuous routine, Woodward and Bernstein find clues to the story by seeking
sources outside of the power structure, sources who cannot deliver
the whole story, but contribute many small pieces that must be fitted together in a complex puzzle.

Managing editor Howard Simons (Martin Balsam) derides Woodward and Bernstein for their flat-footed methods and tells fellow
editors that while he was lunching at the exclusive Sans Souci restaurant, a prominent government flack stopped by to mock the *Post*
for its "Watergate fixation." But while Simons initially scoffs at the
Watergate story, as it gathers momentum he tries to shift it to the
National Desk. At a page-one meeting, he alternately dismisses and
covets the story, and his debate with Woodstein-advocate and metro
editor Rosenfeld illuminates the problem with business-as-usual reporting on a story like Watergate:

> *Rosenfeld* [to Bradlee]: Why don't you ask him what he's really say-
> ing? He wants to take the story away from Woodstein and give it to
> the National Desk.
>
> *Simons*: It's just that we've got some experienced guys sitting around
> who know the politicians, who have the contacts.
>
> *Rosenfeld*: You said it—sitting around!

District of Columbia editor Barry Sussman also has misgivings about
the story and the young reporters to whom it has been entrusted. The
fact that established political reporters can't pry information out of
their powerful sources makes him suspicious of Woodward and
Bernstein's story.

> *Sussman*: Ben, this is a dangerous story for this paper. What if your
> boys get it wrong?
>
> *Bradlee*: Then it's our ass, isn't it?
>
> *Sussman*: It's not just that we're using unnamed sources that bothers
> me. Or that everything we print the White House denies. Or that al-
> most no other papers are reprinting our stories. Look, there are over
> two thousand reporters in this town, are there five on Watergate?
> Where did the *Washington Post* suddenly get the monopoly on wis-
> dom? I don't believe the story. It doesn't make sense.

As the real scandal unfolded, other editors began paying attention
to the *Post*'s Watergate coverage and at least one, Jack Nelson, the
Washington bureau chief for the *Los Angeles Times*, understood that
his troops were lagging on the story because they were relying on their
connections instead of tenaciously tracking leads outside of the official loop. In frustration, Nelson hung a cryptic sign—GOYAKOD—

in the Washington bureau to chastise and inspire his staff. When someone asked Nelson what the sign meant, he explained: *Get Off Your Ass: Knock On Doors.*

In the film, while Woodward and Bernstein do some of their investigating over the phone, they leave the newsroom to find the story instead of expecting it to find them. They knock on doors. When they receive a tip that a White House aide is investigating Ted Kennedy and has checked out materials about Kennedy from the Library of Congress, the duo tries to find out more. The lead fizzles when a librarian who originally confirmed the tip changes her story under pressure from higher-ups. Another librarian tells the reporters they cannot see a list of requests for materials from the White House. An average reporter would turn back at any of these obstacles, but not Woodstein. Since the White House requests are filed with all of the other requests made at the Library of Congress, the pair sifts through every request made over a two-year period, a feat whose futility is illustrated by the director's overhead shot of the two reporters at work in the library. Ultimately, the story proves to be a dead end, but not until the reporters have exhausted every possible means of confirming it.

CANARY IN A COAL MINE

The investigative journalist George Seldes, whose exposures of government duplicity in the 1940s and 1950s (notably about secret atomic weapons testing) went largely unnoticed because he was not affiliated with a mass-circulation, mainstream publication, titled his autobiography *Tell the Truth and Run*. As a gadfly on the margins of political discourse, the best Seldes could do was drop an explosive revelation at the edge of public debate and hope someone who had the public's attention would hear the blast. Mainstream, mass-circulation publications, on the other hand, try to fill the role of steady public mediator. The stories they publish have wide repercussions.

Ethicists argue that journalists must consider the well being of the community when preparing the news report. A drumbeat of conflict, violence, and cynicism, even when supported by accurate stories, can disorient and demoralize a community. Conflict is a prime ingredient of news stories, but publications that focus on conflict to the exclusion of consensus or solutions offer a distorted vision of the community. Many blame the Watergate scandal for diminishing public trust in government and fostering cynicism. Clearly, however, the larger interests of the community were served by the exposure of Watergate. Had Watergate not been exposed, the Nixon White House might have weakened the Constitution and accelerated a pattern of partisan usurpation of the electoral process.

Ironically, despite the suspense of the investigation, it finally stalls and it is up to Deep Throat to explain the significance of the conspiracy. "The cover-up had little do with the Watergate. It was mainly to protect covert operations. It leads everywhere. Get out your notebook. There's more. Your lives are in danger."

The details of the conspiracy provided by Deep Throat made for earthshaking stories and helped to flush out more information about the White House's illegal practices by the *Post* and other publications. The Justice Department could no longer make perfunctory inquiries about White House and CREEP activities. Prosecutors and judges increased the ferocity of their efforts to get to the bottom of Watergate. The *Washington Post* and its two young reporters were the catalysts that sparked the system into action. Ultimately, President Nixon resigned when it became clear a legal noose was tightening around him. Despite the vague threats to their lives that Deep Throat warned of, Woodward and Bernstein not only escaped official retribution, but also became heroes and cultural icons.

As the Watergate cover-up crumbled, presidential spokesman Ron Nessen was forced to concede that "mistakes were made" (a rather disingenuous phrase that omits responsibility for those "mistakes"). The *Post*'s Watergate exposé made, for a few brief shining moments, heroes of the men and women of the press, an institution whose credibility and trustworthiness has fallen steadily in readers' eyes ever since. Reporters began to rip into other institutions, many hoping to bag a major official as Woodstein had. The book the pair wrote, and the film that followed, created a personal celebrity for them that nearly eclipsed the substance of their accomplishments.

More than a quarter-century after Nixon's resignation, the press is fusing into a multimedia information machine, and few big organizations seem eager to undertake the kind of hard-nosed investigative reporting that characterized Watergate. Worse, news organizations today often cynically use the trappings of the investigative genre. Few stories in the past decades have come close to the *Post*'s coverage of Watergate in commitment or scope. Led by the example of Gannett's *USA Today*, newspapers are trying to stave off obsolescence by producing "reader-friendly" stories that speak to readers more as consumers than as citizens—an economic factor that will be explored in chapter 9 concerning the film *Network*. Television news magazines have proliferated, but focus primarily on features or investigative targets that are pitifully modest. Television news broadcasts are stuffed with special features on health, nutrition, science, finance, and quick sound bites.

Despite some of the depressing news about the state of investigative reporting, Watergate continues to inspire and to offer a model of methodical, dedicated reporting on both individual and institutional levels. In addition, Web-based publications—some electronic siblings of newspapers, some independent—offer citizens unprecedented access to the goings-on of government and business. A thriving alternative press continues to expose governmental and corporate wrongdoing. But the major, mainstream news outlets, after an orgy of inquiry following Watergate, have largely pulled back. That might not be all bad. A full-court press is required when crises loom, but relentless investigations into the mundane serve to deaden any outrage we might feel when real threats to our liberties occur. Incessant investigation creates a stasis of cynicism and distrust toward both press and government.

In the late nineteenth century, magazine journalists exposed the perfidies of big government, the tyranny of big business, corruption in the Senate, and exploitation and disease in the meat-packing plants. Reporters writing for *Everybody's Magazine*, *Collier's*, *McClure's*, and other publications stirred outrage among reformers and citizens and their stories led to hearings and reforms. But their day passed. The public became numb to the shock of never-ending revelations and the institutions the journalists attacked fought back. President Theodore Roosevelt, an early admirer of the reformer-journalists, implored them to expose what was good in American life as well as what was bad. He dubbed them "muckrakers," after a character in *Pilgrim's Progress* who was so absorbed in stirring up mud and waste that he could not look up to see the face of God.

The *Post*-Watergate sleuths similarly wore out their welcome. But their day may come again. Ten years before Watergate, it would have been inconceivable that a major newspaper would pursue presidential misconduct with the ardor Woodward and Bernstein displayed. The press supported American involvement in Vietnam almost without question for a decade before the government's lies became too big and too bold to ignore.

When a crisis arises, the press may yet shake off its contented slumber and act as a watchdog. The young reporters likely to lead the next crusade will have to make hard choices about what methods are morally acceptable even when a story is as big and as significant as Watergate. The only way to discover whether such a story exists, however, was plainly spelled out by the *Los Angeles Times*'s Jack Nelson—Get Off Your Ass: Knock On Doors.

QUESTIONS TO CONSIDER

1. Would you conceal or lie about your identity as a reporter to get a big story? Is there a difference between concealment and deception? Explain what circumstances might tempt you to do either and try to justify your actions.

2. How would you feel if you chatted with an attractive stranger in the student union and awoke the next day to see your words in the student newspaper? What if you had said things you would not have said in a public setting where others could overhear?

3. Is it wrong for reporters to snoop through private corporate records to get information about news subjects? *All the President's Men* was made decades before the advent of the Internet; it is much easier now than ever to acquire such information. Would you hack into a Web site to get private information about a company or government agency you suspected of wrongdoing? Is it ethical to publish personal information obtained on the Web even if it is obtained legally?

4. Consider how Bernstein talks his way into the home of the reluctant bookkeeper. Is there anything dishonest in his actions, or is he merely being tenacious and using his considerable powers of persuasion?

5. Do you believe Woodward and Bernstein's attempts to befriend embattled CREEP official Hugh Sloan and his wife were sincere? Should reporters befriend, or pretend to befriend, sources?

6. Are public figures allowed private moments? Nixon aide Ken Clawson shares an off-duty drink with a *Post* reporter. He discloses to her that he wrote a false, but devastating, letter to scuttle the candidacy of Nixon rival Edwin Muskie. Is it ethical of the reporter to tell Woodward and Bernstein of his revelation? Is it ethical of the *Post* to imply that the circumstances of

the revelation—Clawson, a married man, was having a drink in the home of a single woman—might be put in print if he does not confirm the story?

7. Public figures like Miami district attorney Dardis often construct barriers to keep the public and the press at bay. Are reporters and citizens permitted to sneak past those barriers, as Bernstein does by using a ruse to lure Dardis's secretary from her desk?

8. If deceptions like ones employed by Woodward and Bernstein lead us to the truth, are we justified in using them?

FURTHER READING

Bernstein, Carl, and Bob Woodward. *All the President's Men*. New York: Touchstone, 1974.

Bradlee, Ben. *A Good Life: Newspapering and Other Adventures*. New York: Simon and Schuster, 1995.

Cohen, Elliot D., and Deni Elliott, eds. *Journalism Ethics: A Reference Handbook*. Santa Barbara, Calif.: ABC–CLIO, 1997.

Jefferson, Thomas. *Thomas Jefferson on Constitutional Issues: Selected Writings 1787–1825*. Comp. Nobel E. Cunningham Jr. Richmond: Virginia Commission on Constitutional Government, 1962.

Lambeth, Edmund B. *Committed Journalism: An Ethic for the Profession*. Bloomington: Indiana University Press, 1986.

Merrill, John C., and S. Jack Odell. *Philosophy and Journalism*. New York: Longman, 1983.

Nolan, John. "Reporter Admits Taking Voice Mail from Chiquita." *USA Today*, 25 September 1998, 7-A.

Olasky, Marvin. *Central Ideas in the Development of American Journalism: A Narrative History*. Hillsdale, N.J.: Erlbaum, 1991.

Paterno, Sue. "The Lying Game." *American Journalism Review* (May 1997): 40.

Seldes, George. *Tell the Truth and Run*. New York: Greenberg, 1953.

Sumner, David E. "Good Story, Bad Journalism." (Food Lion Case) *Editor and Publisher*, 19 April 1997, 48.

Wills, Gary, ed. *Thomas Jefferson: Genius of Liberty*. New York: Viking Studio in association with the Library of Congress, 2000.

Yarbrough, Jean M. *American Virtues: Thomas Jefferson on the Character of a Free People*. Lawrence: University Press of Kansas, 1998.

4

Under Fire:
The Art of War

In the 1983 film *Under Fire*, Russell Price, a veteran war photographer played by Nick Nolte, finally comes to realize the horrors of war while photographing the Sandinista revolution in Nicaragua. The sight of mangled corpses lying in pools of blood, of refugees plodding down dusty highways, and of baby-faced revolutionaries battling tanks with rocks and bottles stirs his emotions despite his having seen hundreds of similar sights before. For the first time in his long, award-winning career, he is suddenly torn between his responsibility as a journalist to record the truth and his responsibility as a human being to help the underdog.

Director Roger Spottiswoode told the *New York Times* when *Under Fire* was released that the film is "about the complexities of journalism, about journalists coping with the difficulties of being objective and yet having feelings and sensitivities about their subjects." Out of sympathy for the Nicaraguan people, Price becomes a participant in a war he is supposed to be objectively covering. He agrees to a Sandinista request to falsify a news photo, making their dead leader appear to still be alive. The photo serves to bolster the revolution at a key moment. It also serves to bring the whole purpose of journalism into question. Are journalists professional bloodsuckers? How can it be ethical for them to simply watch while others suffer and die? Is objectivity ever worth sacrificing for a higher cause?

Under Fire belongs to a cycle of 1980s films that includes *The Year of Living Dangerously*, *Deadline*, *The Killing Fields*, and *Salvador*. All the films follow, as critic Marek Haltof notes, "the adventures of Western journalists in countries experiencing political and economic turmoil." But *Under Fire* was probably the most controversial of the lot. It romanticized the Sandinistas as freedom fighters at a time when the Reagan administration was demonizing them as tyrants, even worse than Anastasio Somoza, the corrupt, American-backed dictator they deposed in 1979. The National Press Club in Washington, which originally planned to sponsor a screening of *Under Fire*, withdrew after word leaked out that the film suggested that the Sandinista cause was noble and that some press coverage of the revolution had been biased in favor of the rebels.

The issue of bias was real, not just a Hollywood fantasy. It had been raised earlier by Shirley Christian of the *Washington Post*, who had won the 1981 Pulitzer Prize for international reporting for her coverage of Nicaragua after Somoza's fall. In a 1982 article in *Washington Journalism Review*, she claims that the American press, in its eagerness to rid Nicaragua of Somoza and his brutal National Guard, misrepresented or overlooked the Marxist-Leninist ideology of the Sandinistas. She believes that the press's coming face to face with the atrocities of Guardsmen—including the summary execution of ABC correspondent Bill Stewart—made the Sandinistas seem attractive by comparison. Yet what journalists saw, Christian says, may not have been a reign of terror by an especially repressive regime, but the horrors of any kind of war. She accuses the press of going on a "guilt trip" in Nicaragua, the legacy of a half-century of U.S. mistakes there.

In *Under Fire*, Price goes on a guilt trip of his own, altering a photo in a bid to alter the course of history. But before we condemn him for falling away from the truth, we should perhaps remember something contemporary philosopher David Nyberg has written: "Truth-telling is a value that is likely to exist in conflict with many others—kindness, compassion, self-regard, privacy, survival, and so on." It isn't always easy to determine which value should take precedence when; there is no one-size-fits-all standard for ethical choices. Nonetheless, as Price discovers, we still have to somehow choose.

PICTURE THIS

Photojournalists cover subjects ranging from hard news (wars, floods, accidents) to features (food, fashion, ground-breakings). As Kenneth Kobre points out in *Photojournalism: The Professionals' Approach*, the ethics of staging a photograph often turns on which role the photojournalist is playing on any given assignment—reporter or artist with a camera. Most experts agree that when it comes to hard-news situations, photojournalists should not manipulate images. "No image used in the news," Philip Patterson and Lee Wilkins assert, "is ethical unless it treats the subjects or topics fairly and attempts to present an accurate and unambiguous picture of reality." Echoes Andy Grundberg, a frequent writer on photography for the *New York Times*: "In the realm of news, clarity, brevity, and objectivity are held to be guiding virtues, and images that express overtly personal points of view are unwelcome." He adds that even in the hands of legendary photojournalists Robert Capa and W. Eugene Smith, who were "partisans of social change and to an extent rebels against the publishing system, photojournalism boiled down to the need to produce clear and immediate images that the average reader could readily grasp."

At the beginning of *Under Fire*, Price is in the central African nation of Chad, covering a civil war and apparently living up to these tough professional standards. He repeatedly risks his skin to get dramatic pictures of a helicopter gunship strafing an elephant convoy, the action on the screen freezing in exotic tableaus whenever he clicks the camera. One of the shots is later reproduced, to general admiration, as a cover of *Time* magazine.

Yet for all Price's ability and courage, something is lacking in his work, some understanding of his subjects. "How is it," Grundberg wonders, "that we can expect an outsider—the ambulatory photojournalist, a glorified tourist—to deliver essential insights into a foreign culture?" He notes that most photojournalists "come from comfortable backgrounds in the West" and that "their efforts to describe the Third World can be criticized as a kind of visual imperialism." Certainly, *Under Fire* criticizes their efforts as such. It shows Price and his colleagues merrily jetting from crisis to crisis, where they have exciting adventures and profit professionally from war, misery, and death.

In other words, they are hedonists. The philosophy of hedonism was founded by a student of Socrates, Aristippus, who died in Athens in 366 B.C. Aristippus believed that people should dedicate their lives to pleasure and not worry about the future. He was referring, however, to "pleasures of the mind—intellectual pleasures." Modern usage has distorted his original meaning. Today hedonism is the justifying philosophy of the ambitious, the greedy, and the opportunistic. The journalists in *Under Fire* fall into this category.

Consider the fact that Price makes sexual advances to radio reporter Claire Stryder (Joanna Cassidy) even though she is involved with senior *Time* correspondent Alex Grazier (Gene Hackman), his best friend. Also consider how much the journalists in the film resemble, to borrow Grundberg's metaphor, glorified tourists, keenly interested in the Club Med aspects of the countries they cover. "I hear it's a neat little war with a nice hotel," Grazier says of Nicaragua, the next stop on the press's itinerary of third world hot spots. When Price arrives there sometime after his colleagues, he is anxious to get caught up. "Give me the scoop on Nicaragua," he asks Stryder. She begins to recount its political history. "No," Price interrupts, "I don't mean the peasant stuff. I mean the real stuff. Come on." Stryder smiles and says, "Well, there are two kinds of beer. . . ."

The film draws a parallel between the journalists and a viciously amoral, apolitical American mercenary named Oates (Ed Harris), who keeps crossing their path. In fact, while still in Chad, Oates recommends Nicaragua to Price in terms he can understand: "Nicaragua, that's the spot. Cheap shrimp, a lot of rays, and not too heavy in the spook department." Both Price and Oates are professional crisis-chasers, but Price shoots pictures and Oates shoots people. Later, even this distinction begins to blur when Oates uses Price's personal file of unpublished photos, stolen from his hotel room, to identify rebels for execution.

Writing in *Film Quarterly*, James Roy MacBean recalls that photos have long been used by the state to monitor political dissent. In 1871, when Paris newspapers published photos of the crowds gathered in the streets to hear the leaders of the Commune spouting revolution, the police used the pictures to round up both the leaders and many of their listeners. But, for Price, the realization that photos can lend themselves to partisan uses comes late and as a rude and bitter shock.

Price arrives in Nicaragua practicing the photojournalist's credo of neutrality—the idea that a photo, in Patterson and Wilkins's words, "should be as objective a picture of reality as technology will allow." He brings with him not knowledge of the country or concern for its people, but the cold, implacable curiosity of the hired observer. His main interest lies in scooping the world by taking the first-ever photo of Commandante Rafael, leader of the Sandinista guerrillas. "Anyone crazy enough to look for him," Grazier warns, "is gonna get his nuts shot off." This only further encourages the intrepid Price. In one scene, after he is beaten by National Guardsmen and tossed in a jail cell with a priest accused of knowing Rafael, his thoughts immediately revert to the desired photo despite his battered condition.

Price: I would like to find Rafael myself.

Priest: Whose side are you on?

Price: I don't take sides. I take pictures.

Priest: No side?

[Price shakes his head.]

Priest: Go home.

Of course, Price ignores this advice. He stays and gets his scoop, but at what cost?

SEEING IS BELIEVING

The photo Price thinks will be a journalistic coup proves instead to be an ethical dilemma that casts everything he ever believed about his work in doubt. He and Stryder are escorted into the mountains by Sandinistas, who promise that he will be able to take Rafael's picture. "It's a good story. You will be more famous," one of them says. But when Price finally comes face to face with Rafael, the guerrilla leader is dead. The Sandinistas want Price to photograph him in such a way as to make him look alive. They explain that if Somoza can show evidence of success in his fight against the guerrillas—for example, the killing of Rafael—Washington will send him an additional $25 million in arms. The war will drag on, and many more people will die.

Initially, Price rejects taking the proposed photo. "I'm a journalist," he protests. "I don't do things like this." The Sandinistas give him the night to reconsider, and during those dark hours, he and Stryder wrestle with the decision.

> *Stryder*: Do I go back and say I saw Rafael stone-cold dead, or do I go back and say I fell in love with the guerrillas because their cause was. . . .
>
> *Price*: Sympathetic?
>
> *Stryder*: Yeah, sympathetic. Christ, what are we doing here?

In the morning, Price takes the picture. It inspires antigovernment rallies throughout the country when published. The evil Somoza regime begins to crumble.

Did Price behave ethically? Can we somehow excuse or justify his resort to deception? The answer may depend on how we define the role-related responsibilities of a photojournalist. Are these primarily to the viewers of his or her photos or the subjects of them?

"The impact of a visual image on a viewer," Paul Martin Lester writes in *Photojournalism: An Ethical Approach*, stems "from the belief that 'the camera never lies,'" that the image captures reality. Or, as Grundberg wryly puts it, "One would assume that photographs are more reliable representations of historical events than, say, cave drawings or hieroglyphics." But the assumption may be unwarranted. In a strange paradox, the very "truthfulness" of photography—its apparent ability to offer direct access to the real—provides the basis for deceiving a credulous public. And there is a long history of photojournalists doing just that through the manipulation or fabrication of images.

Many pictures taken during the Spanish-American War, for example, were staged. Battle scenes were reenacted (sometimes in New Jersey backyards), and dead bodies rearranged for better compositions. During World War I, newspapers printed fake propaganda photos of German atrocities, including some of Kaiser Wilhelm II cutting the hands off babies. Even the Pulitzer Prize–winning picture of U.S. Marines planting the flag on Iwo Jima in World War II, perhaps the most famous photo to come out of any war, is rumored to have been posed by Associated Press photographer Joe Rosenthal.

Precisely because the photographic image is such an unstable item—"Images can lie outright:" Susan Moeller notes, "They can be published with misleading captions, they can be morphed on computers"—photojournalists need to reflect on the ethical dimension of their work. The consensus among experts is that "while art may be manipulated, information may not." At a symposium on photojournalism at Northwestern University in 1991, a student in the audience asked Phil Greer, director of photography for the *Chicago Tribune*, "When is it permissible to alter a news photo?" "Never," thundered Greer, leaning over the rostrum and jamming his finger toward the questioner, "never!" In a similar vein but milder tone, Patterson and Wilkins advise, "Don't deceive an audience that expects your pictures to be an accurate representation of a particular quality of reality."

By these strict standards, Price's picture of Rafael is unethical. It is also unethical, apparently, according to a simple test devised by photo editor Elizabeth Biondi. She suggests that photojournalists consider whether they would feel comfortable writing a note to readers explaining how this or that picture was taken. If the photojournalist is willing for readers to know the circumstances, then the picture is probably ethically acceptable. Now let's observe Price. In the scene where Grazier guesses that the Rafael picture is a fake, Price becomes extremely agitated, seeming to fear public exposure and professional ruin.

So is there nothing that can be said in favor of his decision to help the Sandinistas with some creative photography? Perhaps there is— if we redefine his role-related responsibilities. "Individuals who hold power over another, whether it is . . . within the professional-client or professional-community relationship," media ethicist Deni Elliott points out, "have special responsibilities in regard to those who are vulnerable to them." As a photojournalist, Price has power over readers, which he supposedly abuses when he manipulates the photographic image. But doesn't he also have power over the people recorded by his camera—the soldiers, the refugees, the wounded— and doesn't this give him certain responsibilities to them, too? Art critic John Berger would argue that it does and that these responsibilities actually take precedence. The ethical photojournalist, in Berger's opinion, would think of him- or herself "not so much as a reporter to the rest of the world but . . . as a recorder for those involved in the events photographed."

Kevin Carter was one photojournalist who felt burdened by the often painful images he caught on film. In 1993 Carter took a picture of a well-fed vulture threatening a starving Sudanese girl who had collapsed on the road to an aid station. He sat under a tree after shooting the picture and smoked a cigarette and cried. "I couldn't distance myself from the horrors of what I saw," he said. His picture would raise world consciousness of famine in Africa as well as win a Pulitzer Prize. But two months after accepting the award, the thirty-three-year-old Carter connected a hose to the exhaust pipe of his red Toyota pickup truck and gassed himself to death. He had earlier told a friend, "I'm really, really sorry I didn't pick the child up." Susan Moeller, commenting in 1999 on Carter's suicide, writes: "Being close enough to photograph the starving child meant being close enough to help. The responsibility to bear witness does not automatically outweigh the responsibility to be involved." Just ask Price.

DARKNESS BURNING

Violence, disorder, disease, and death are mainstays of news coverage, especially foreign news coverage. The assumption in most newsrooms is that Americans aren't interested in foreign news unless it is dramatic or violent. A 1995 study by the Pew Research Center for the People and the Press found that fully 40 percent of foreign news was conflict-driven.

A scene in *Under Fire* suggests just how difficult it can be to get the American press to pay attention to foreign events. The rebels have blown up a nightclub in Managua—significant because it is the first sign that the fighting has spread to the Nicaraguan capital. *Time* magazine nonetheless balks at publishing the story. "Alex, it's Charlie in New York," an assistant, phone in hand, yells across the pressroom. "He says the nightclub bombing isn't big enough to hold for the 'World' section." Grazier stops typing, thinks for a moment, then yells back, "Tell him there were pieces of body in the piano and some of them were singing 'Moonlight in Vermont.' What's he got better than that?"

Although always a hard sell, foreign news is more likely to be published or broadcast if accompanied by sensational pictures. "Images of trauma," Moeller notes, "have become intrinsic to the marketing of the media. Papers are laid out, newsmagazine covers are chosen, television news is packaged to make the most of emotional images of crises." But simply because a picture is commercially justifiable doesn't mean it is ethically so. Today, when violent images abound in the media, often the only justification for running them involves their impact, the power of the images to provoke fear or grief or pity. As Eric Meskauskas, photo editor of the *New York Daily News*, states, "Since we've seen almost everything there is to see in this age, what photo editors are trying to do is make you feel something." The problem is, the more images of suffering and death you see, the less you may actually come to feel.

Moeller devotes an entire book to this paradox. In it, she contends that how the media typically cover crises—by running and rerunning the worst scenes of violence and tragedy—produces a condition called "compassion fatigue." "Too much harping on the same set of images," she claims, "too much strident coverage with insufficient background and context, exhaust the public." Rather than being educated or emotionally moved by crisis coverage, the public becomes callused. They turn away in boredom.

If this kind of coverage wears out the public, just think what it must do to the photojournalists who help provide it. "Within a few years on the job," Lester states, "a photojournalist learns all the ways people die—drownings, car and plane crashes, murders, and many mind-numbing accidents. And as with others who witness such events—police, fire and ambulance workers, nurses, and doctors—post-traumatic stress disorder or 'battle fatigue' effects [*sic*] photojournalists." Kevin Carter, the Pulitzer Prize–winning photographer who took his own life, is a tragic example. In his suicide note, he wrote, "I am haunted by the vivid memories of killings & corpses & anger & pain . . . of starving or wounded children, of trigger-happy madmen."

The same terrible ghosts come to haunt Price in *Under Fire*. "Alex," he says, trying to justify his phony picture, "I think I finally saw one too many bodies." His case seems to confirm a remark of Lester's: "A photographer who shoots too many stressful assignments that conflict with an ethical philosophy runs the risk of catching career burnout." Unlike Lester, however, the film implies that burnout can have positive aspects. Price doesn't so much go to pieces as piece things together in a new way. He may lose his professional poise, but he finds his connection to suffering humanity and, for the first time, realizes that the lives and deaths of real people are involved in the events he photographs.

This realization reflects Kantian ethics. Immanuel Kant formulated three versions of the Categorical Imperative, his name for the ultimate moral norm. Kant preferred the first version, "Act on the maxim that you will to become a universal law," but thought that the wording of the second and third might be clearer to his readers. It is the second version, called the Formula of Respect for the Dignity of Persons, that is most applicable to Price: "Act so that you treat humanity, whether in your own person or in that of any other, always as an end and never as a means only."

Until Nicaragua, Price regarded the conflicts he covered with purely professional interest, unconcerned about which side was right, which side wrong, happy just to shoot compelling images. He treated the subjects of his pictures instrumentally, as a means to his career goals—bigger publications, higher fees, and greater fame. The Sandinistas who promise him a chance to take the first-ever photo of Rafael consciously play on his vanity and ambition, assuring him, "You'll be more famous." But somewhere along the way Price develops the capacity to feel another culture. He begins to sympathize with the rebels, many of them still teenagers, in their fight against the murderer Somoza. His Rafael photo, fake though it is, represents a humane gesture, his attempt to contribute to the welfare of others.

The second version of the Categorical Imperative is described by Roger J. Sullivan as "an ethics for relations between strangers," but it also outlines our duty to ourselves. Our worth doesn't depend on our usefulness or desirability, Kant says. Each of us has intrinsic value by virtue of being a person. Unfortunately, in manipulating a photo at the urging of the Sandinistas, Price treats himself instrumentally. He becomes merely a tool, a thing, a means to somebody else's end. And so even after awakening to the humanity of his photographic subjects, he seems an ethically questionable figure, standing half in the light, half in the dark, and all in a messy universe.

TRUTH OR CONSEQUENCES

While some might argue that the general messiness of the universe makes the formulation of clear, precise ethical rules all the more important, others might argue that such rules are out of touch with reality and just complicate our actual situation. Perhaps what people need in order to survive or even flourish isn't a set of rigid rules, but flexibility. Frederick the Great, a student of the pragmatic ethics of sixteenth-century political philosopher Niccolò Machiavelli, stated, "If there is anything to be gained by being honest, let us be honest. If it is necessary to deceive, let us deceive."

In *Under Fire*, Price and Stryder find it necessary to deceive. So does Grazier, who leaves Nicaragua to become a TV anchorman in New York, only to return to try to get an interview with Rafael after Price's picture creates a sensation. When Price and Stryder finally admit to him that the photo is a fake and Rafael is dead, he blows his top. "You just served me up your careers," he threatens. "I could bury you." Yet his anger stems more from personal pique ("I'm not just talking about Rafael. That's a lie I despise, but I understand. I'm talking about the two of you lying to me.") than from professional disapproval. Grazier, in fact, never exposes Price and Stryder. At one point, he even lies to protect them. Asked by a correspondent whether the photo is, as rumor now has it, phony, he says no.

Why would Grazier lie like that? It must be because his loyalty to Price and Stryder after years of shared hardship and adventure outweighs his loyalty to the truth. "The test of whether we ought to tell the truth," Nyberg writes in *The Varnished Truth: Truth Telling and Deceiving in Ordinary Life*, "is in getting face to face with somebody in a situation that calls for a choice and directly appreciating the obligations which arise. Truth telling may be one of these obligations. There will be others." Nyberg proposes that we base our choices on John Stuart Mill's Principle of Utility, often summed up as "Bring the greatest happiness to the greatest number." "The most trustworthy sign that something good has been done," he claims, "that the right policy has been chosen, is the happiness, or sense of well-being, or welfare that comes about as a result. If the action produces happiness at not too great a cost, then it is good." Thus, lying is acceptable as long as the lie has a generally positive outcome.

A couple of objections to this notion of beneficial lies spring to mind. First, as Sissela Bok says, "We cannot take for granted the altruism or good judgment of those who lie to us. . . . We have learned that much deceit for private gain masquerades as being in the public interest." American political history since the early 1960s is replete with examples—the Vietnam War, the Watergate scandal, the Iran-Contra affair. Second, it is just not possible for us to accurately project how our actions will affect others. Such omniscience belongs to gods, not to mere humans. Our inability to know or control all the consequences of our actions makes outcome-based ethics extremely problematic.

Under Fire shows why. Bloody events, none of them intended by Price, occur as a result of his conspiring with the Sandinistas. He fakes a photo in the belief it will help topple a foul tyrant and end the war, but it contributes instead to further violence and death. Lured back to Nicaragua by the photo, Grazier is gunned down by National Guard thugs, an echo of the shooting of ABC correspondent Bill

Stewart. Then pictures Price took while he and Stryder were visiting the rebel hideout in the mountains are stolen by a double agent named Jazy (Jean-Louis Trintignant), who passes them on to a government hit squad. Without ever meaning to, Price becomes the finger man for the killings that follow, at least indirectly responsible for the growing pile of torn, blood-splattered corpses.

It is the enigmatic Jazy who, with nervous young Sandinistas pointing guns at his head, underlines for the audience the slipperiness of outcome-based ethics. "You chose the wrong side," Stryder says to him as he is about to be summarily executed. "In twenty years," he replies, "we'll know who's right." But who can wait twenty years to make a choice? If life can only be understood backwards, how do you live forwards?

"The most that any one of us can seem to do," Ernest Becker observes in *The Denial of Death*, "is to fashion something—an object or ourselves—and drop it into the confusion, make an offering of it, so to speak, to the life force." Other philosophers acknowledge that life can be confusing and chaotic, but suggest that we should adhere to certain obligations or rules, regardless. Chief among these obligations for journalists has been truth-telling. Bob Steele, director of the Ethics Program at the Poynter Institute for Media Studies, puts "Seek truth and report it as fully as possible" at the very top of his list of "Guiding Principles for the Journalist." And the obligation is the same whether a journalist reports with a camera or a pen. "A photojournalist who believes in high ethical standards," Lester states, "will not manipulate a subject even slightly. For once a minor manipulation occurs, ethical principles fall like a house of cards."

Yet, at the end of *Under Fire*, Price expresses no guilt or regret about his decision to manipulate an image. He evidently believes that more good than bad resulted from it. Grazier may be dead, but Somoza has slunk off and the rebels have come to power. As Price and Stryder watch a victory celebration in the streets of Managua, she asks, "Did we fall in love with too much?" "I'd do it again," he says. Would you?

QUESTIONS TO CONSIDER

1. Did Grazier have an ethical duty to expose Price and Stryder when he found out that the Rafael picture was phony? Can he somehow balance his duty to old friends, the profession of jour-

nalism, and media users? Is his death connected in any way to poor ethical decision making on his own part?

2. Are there times when a journalist's obligation to tell the truth must yield to other obligations? Was the Nicaraguan revolution one of those times? What other obligations might compete with truth-telling? On what basis should a journalist choose among these obligations?

3. To whom do photojournalists owe primary loyalty, to the subjects of photographs or the viewers of them? Would the pictures now published and broadcast by the media be different if photojournalists felt a stronger loyalty to those photographed? In what ways might they be different? Would that be an improvement? How so?

4. Can doing ethical journalism protect journalists against burnout? Justify your response.

5. Is the classic journalistic pose of objectivity and detachment an obstacle to ethical conduct? Must one's responsibilities as a journalist necessarily clash with one's sympathies as a human being? Can you think of journalists who have remained sympathetic toward their subjects while fulfilling their journalistic responsibilities? Your examples can be contemporary or historical.

6. Do you agree with Becker's statement that "[t]he most that any one of us can seem to do is to fashion something—an object or ourselves—and drop it into the confusion, make an offering of it, so to speak, to the life force"? What kind of "something" would you fashion? Why?

7. Examine the foreign news in a daily newspaper or on a half-hour newscast. How much foreign news is there? Does it mostly involve conflict and tragedy? Is it accompanied by sensational images? Is regular exposure to such news coverage likely to educate media users or desensitize them? Does the press have an ethical responsibility to present foreign news in a different format?

8. The second version of Kant's Categorical Imperative reads, "Act so that you treat humanity, whether in your own person or in that of any other, always as an end and never as a means only." Discuss how, if taken seriously by journalists, this ethical precept might affect one of the following: reporter-source, reporter-audience, or reporter-editor relations.

FURTHER READING

Becker, Ernest. *The Denial of Death*. New York: The Free Press, 1973.

Bernstein, Richard. "Issues Raised by 'Under Fire.'" *New York Times*, 30 October 1983, B9–10.

Bok, Sissela. *Lying: Moral Choice in Public and Private Life*. New York: Pantheon, 1978.

Christian, Shirley. "Covering the Sandinistas." *Washington Journalism Review* (March 1982): 33–38.

Elliott, Deni. "Ethical and Moral Responsibilities of the Media." In *Images That Injure: Pictorial Stereotypes in the Media*, ed. Paul Martin Lester. Westport, Conn.: Praeger, 1996.

Grundberg, Andy. *Crisis of the Real: Writings on Photography Since 1974*. New York: Aperture, 1999.

Haltof, Marek. *Peter Weir: When Cultures Collide*. New York: Twayne, 1996.

Kelly, Tom. "Manipulating Reality." *Editor and Publisher*, 8 June 1991, 16–17.

Kobre, Kenneth. *Photojournalism: The Professionals' Approach*. 3rd ed. Boston: Focal, 1996.

Lester, Paul Martin. *Photojournalism: An Ethical Approach*. Hillsdale, N.J.: Erlbaum, 1991.

MacBean, James Roy. "Watching the Third World Watchers." *Film Quarterly* 37 (1984): 3–13.

Matloff, Judith. "The Legacy of Kevin Carter: Eye on Apartheid." *Columbia Journalism Review* (November–December 1994): 57–60.

Moeller, Susan. *Compassion Fatigue: How the Media See Disease, Famine, War and Death*. New York: Routledge, 1999.

Nyberg, David. *The Varnished Truth: Truth Telling and Deceiving in Ordinary Life*. Chicago: University of Chicago Press, 1992.

Patterson, Philip, and Lee Wilkins, eds. *Media Ethics: Issues and Cases*. 3rd ed. Boston: McGraw-Hill, 1998.

Poynter Institute for Media Studies, <http://www.poynter.org>

Sullivan, Roger J. *An Introduction to Kant's Ethics*. Cambridge: Cambridge University Press, 1994.

5

The Paper:
Boxing with the Truth

Two white businessmen are found shot to death execution-style in a parked car in Brooklyn. When police arrest two black teenage boys in the killings, the media pounce on the story. The *New York Sun*, a tough-talking tabloid with a genius for the sensational, plans to play the arrests on the front page under the incriminating headline "GOTCHA!" Then metro editor Henry Hackett (Michael Keaton) receives a tip that the boys have been framed. He wants to hold the presses in order to investigate further. Managing editor Alicia Clark (Glenn Close) resists. A delay will cost the paper, perpetually teetering on the edge of bankruptcy, thousands of dollars. She says go with the story as is—if it is wrong, it can be fixed tomorrow. Meanwhile, the clock races toward deadline.

This is the situation in *The Paper*, a 1994 film written by brothers David and Stephen Koepp and directed by Ron Howard. To help us compare the merits of Hackett's and Clark's respective positions, we will use the Potter Box, a decision-making model named for its originator, Ralph B. Potter of the Harvard Divinity School. Developed in the 1960s to analyze the debate over nuclear-arms policy, the Potter Box has since been applied to issues ranging from population control to health care to news coverage. Arthur C. Dyck, a Harvard colleague of Potter's, states that the Potter Box can "refurbish and upgrade moral reasoning with respect both to what characteristics of situations will be regarded as right- or wrong-making and what criteria will serve to render our moral judgments reasonable, so that we act in concert with . . . our own deeply held values and so that these values, in turn, are subjected to self-conscious scrutiny."

The Potter Box has four distinct but interrelated steps: (1) outlining the facts of the case; (2) identifying the values at stake; (3) appealing to a moral principle; and (4) choosing a loyalty (see fig. 5.1).

Beginning in the upper left-hand corner, you proceed toward a decision by moving counterclockwise through the box. Clifford G. Christians, Kim B. Rotzoll, and Mark Fackler note in *Media Ethics: Cases and Moral Reasoning* that "the process by which choices are made is of the greatest importance." The Potter Box is designed to ensure that all the relevant factors in a decision—facts, values, principles, and loyalties—will be considered and given appropriate weight.

In this chapter, we will go step by step through the Potter Box in an effort to determine what was the best way for the *Sun* to handle

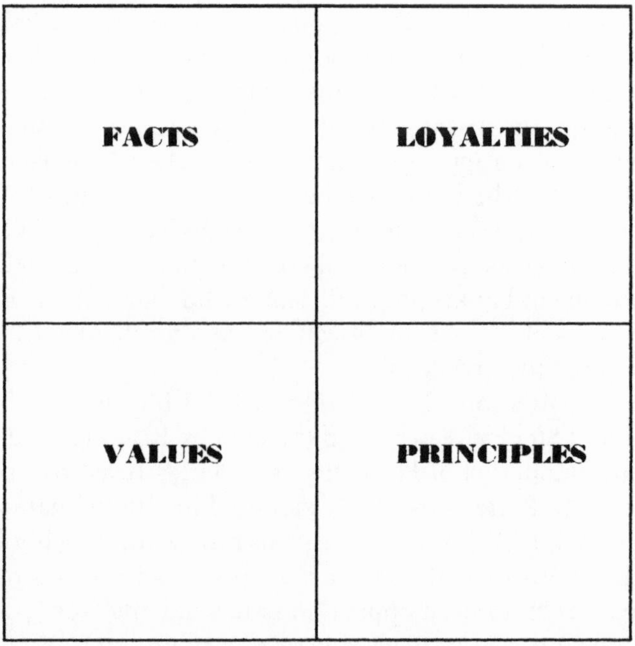

FACTS	**LOYALTIES**
VALUES	**PRINCIPLES**

Figure 5.1   The Potter Box

the arrest story. If Hackett and Clark had gone through these steps, their disagreement might never have degenerated into snarls and insults and, finally, a fistfight. The Potter Box doesn't eliminate differences, but at the very least it elevates them to the philosophical realm.

FACTS

Most of the key facts in the case have already been outlined, but a few more bear mentioning. First, the city is crackling with racial tension, and inflammatory news coverage could spark a riot. Second, the person to whom Hackett and Clark would usually appeal for mediation or advice, executive editor Bernie White (Robert Duvall), has just been diagnosed with cancer and won't be available to play referee. Third, both Hackett and Clark have various other things weighing on their minds and perhaps affecting the quality of their decision making.

Hackett is still smarting over having been scooped by the competition on the story of the double murder. He also has a job interview this afternoon with the *New York Sentinel*, a snooty, conservative paper reminiscent of the *New York Times*. The job would mean higher pay and better hours, and his wife, Martha Hackett (Marisa Tomei), a reporter on maternity leave, is pressuring him to take it. But his secretary asks, "Do you really want to count pencils uptown? Is that you?" He isn't sure.

As for Clark, her central preoccupation seems to be herself. "Do you think my job is easy?" she whines with self-pity. "Do you think it's fun to fire people?" Although she forces severe economies on the newsroom staff, she personally spends more than she earns, admitting at one point, "I got financial problems that make Russia look well managed." On top of that, she is vain, pinching the skin at her wrists for telltale signs of flab; greedy, demanding a raise or to be let out of her contract; and unfaithful, betraying her husband with the editor of the features department.

Are these all the facts worth considering? Some ethicists recommend that once you reach a decision in a case, you go around the Potter Box again, this time including the possible consequences of your decision as part of the facts. By doing so, you might be able to avoid moral tragedy, which occurs, Dyck says, "when, after you have acted in a certain way and reflected on how you have acted, you come to the conclusion that . . . had you thought about it before you acted, you would have acted differently."

VALUES

Next, we must sort out the values involved. Values here refer to those things we consider desirable. "When you value something," Philip Patterson and Lee Wilkins explain in *Media Ethics: Issues and Cases*, "it means you are willing to give up other things for it. . . . An important element of the Potter Box is to be honest about what you really do value." We need to ask what Clark values that she would plunge ahead with publication even though the arrest story might be untrue, or what Hackett values that he would hold up publication at the risk of costing the paper tens of thousands of dollars.

On the one hand, Clark chiefly values the bottom line. "What are you," Hackett rages during one of their many shouting matches, "market research all of a sudden? Not everything is about money." To which Clark replies: "It is when you almost fold every six months." She is a hard-faced, cold-hearted corporate type, as much an accountant as a journalist, who takes professional pride in the fact that she can publish with 350 people the kind of paper it requires *Newsday* 700 people to publish. Her values reek of the desire for money and power and for the special status that money and power can confer.

On the other hand, Hackett values truth and fairness more than profits or efficiency. At the 3 P.M. budget meeting—the meeting where editors decide the play of stories—he tells the group about receiving a tip that the arrests are bogus.

Clark: It's a great lead. We'll follow it up tomorrow, but without a confirmation, we'll still run GOTCHA!

Hackett: What if they aren't the guys? What if they're innocent?

Clark: We taint 'em today, we make 'em look good on Saturday. Everybody's happy.

[The other editors laugh in cynical agreement.]

Hackett: Wait a minute. This is a story that could permanently alter the public's perception of two teenagers who might be innocent and, as a weekend bonus, ignite another race war. How about that?

The conflict between Hackett and Clark over the story reflects a deeper conflict in values. "A forthright articulation of all of the values wrapped up in any particular ethical situation," Patterson and

Wilkins write, "will help you see more clearly the choices that you face and the potential compromises you may or may not have to make." But has Hackett been completely forthright in articulating his values? Clark doesn't believe so. "Oh, come on, Henry," she says, "you don't care if [the teenagers] got [framed] or not. That's not what this is all about. We got our asses kicked yesterday, so you want to beat everyone else today, that's all." "Yeah," Hackett admits, "I do, I do." He values scoops, then, in addition to truth and fairness. There is nothing inherently wrong with this. It is only a problem if he gets carried away by his competitive zeal. Unfortunately, as we will later examine, perhaps he does get carried away, swept into dark places journalists shouldn't go.

PRINCIPLES

In this step, we appeal to a recognized ethical principle. Christians, Rotzoll, and Fackler insist that "no conclusion can be morally justified without a clear demonstration that an ethical principle shaped the final decision." The principle might be a formal statement of moral philosophy, such as Immanuel Kant's Categorical Imperative ("Act on that maxim which you will to become a universal law") or John Stuart Mill's Principle of Utility ("Bring the greatest happiness to the greatest number"). Or it might be something more homely and familiar, the kind of moral aphorisms on which many of us were raised: Do no harm, tell the truth, protect the innocent.

As we have seen, Hackett bases his argument for delaying presstime on notions of truth and fairness. Both truth-telling and fairness are foundational principles of modern journalism, enshrined in the profession's various codes of ethics. For example, the SPJ's Code of Ethics, adopted in 1996, states under the heading "Seek Truth and Report It" that "[j]ournalists should be honest, fair and courageous in gathering, reporting and interpreting information." The Radio-Television News Directors Association's (RTNDA) Code of Broadcast Ethics similarly urges members to "[s]trive to present the source or nature of broadcast news material in a way that is balanced, accurate and fair."

But none of this seems to matter to Clark. She makes not the slightest attempt to morally justify her decision to go with "GOTCHA!" on the front page. Mortimer J. Adler, a great popularizer of philosophical ideas, writes in *Desires Right and Wrong: The Ethics of*

Enough that "there are many, perhaps even a majority among the educated and sophisticated, whose wrong thinking avoids or dismisses all moral problems. For them, there are only practical problems—problems of success or expediency in getting what they want." Clark is apparently one of these people. She defends her decision making—when she deigns to defend it at all—on practical rather than principled grounds. Of chief concern to her isn't truth or fairness, but the fact that it costs $12,000 every half-hour the paper is late.

Questions of journalistic principle ripple through the climactic scene of the film. Hackett and a reporter named McDougal (Randy Quaid) return to the newsroom from Brooklyn with confirmation that the teenagers were framed. They rush in full of enthusiasm and excitement, but suddenly deflate when they realize that the presses are already printing "GOTCHA!" Moments later, down in the noisy, cavernous pressroom, Hackett tries to get Clark to see the situation in ethical terms.

Hackett: Did you run that? Did you run that headline?

Clark: You're goddamn right I did.

Hackett: It's wrong. It's a hundred-eighty degrees wrong. We got to change it.

Clark [to a pressman]: How far are we into the run?

Pressman: Quarter of the way, maybe more. There's ninety thousand papers on the street.

Clark [to Hackett]: Oh, no way, no way. We run what we got.

Hackett: It's wrong.

Clark: Given the information we had at the time, the story's right.

Hackett: Yeah, but it's not right. I got a cop. I got a quote. It's wrong.

Clark: Not for today it's not. Tomorrow it's wrong. We only have to be right for a day.

Hackett: This shouldn't be semantics. This shouldn't be money. People will read this, Alicia, and they'll believe us.

Clark: We're the *Sun*. They'll take us with a grain of salt. We'll run yours tomorrow.

Hackett: No, no, not tomorrow. Right fucking now. Today.

Clark [in a tone of finality to the pressman]: We run what we got.

It is Clark's argument that the *Sun* has, as a cheesy tabloid, less duty to respect the truth than do traditional broadsheets like the *New York Times* and the *Washington Post*. Beginning in 1919 with the founding of the *New York Daily News*, the first tabloid newspaper in the United States, tabloids have been associated with some of the worst features of the American press, from lurid coverage of crime, sex, and scandal to sports mania to mindless celebrity worship. But while tabloids may be guilty of misplaced emphasis and sensationalism, most rarely lie outright. McDougal makes just this point in a conversation with Clark at a bar after work.

Clark: We're not exactly the *Washington Post*, okay?

McDougal: No, no, we're not. We run stupid headlines because we think they're funny. We run maimings on the front page because we got good art. . . . But at least it's the truth. As far as I can remember we never ever—*ever*—got a story knowingly wrong, until tonight.

A look of poignant thoughtfulness appears on Clark's face. Before the film ends, she will undergo a conversion and order the front page torn up and the real story substituted. "Trust and integrity are precious resources," Sissela Bok states in *Lying: Moral Choice in Public and Private Life*, "easily squandered, hard to regain. They can thrive only on a foundation of respect for veracity." Hackett intuitively knows this. Clark has to learn it.

LOYALTIES

The fourth step in the Potter Box is perhaps the hardest—choosing where our ultimate loyalty lies. Journalists face many legitimate claims on their loyalty. They owe loyalty to their employer, their audience, their profession, and themselves. Often these loyalties conflict, and when they do, journalists must decide which should carry the most weight.

But decide how? Patterson and Wilkins suggest following the lead of Josiah Royce, an early twentieth-century American theologian who viewed loyalty as a social commitment, the "willing and practical and thoroughgoing devotion of a person to a worthy cause." A cause was worthy in Royce's eyes if it contributed to the good of the community.

The only cause Clark considers worthy is her own career. Her hunger for position and power is so intense that she sacrifices the honor of journalism to it. She isn't loyal to the *Sun* (she threatens to quit the paper unless paid more money). She isn't loyal to readers (she knowingly publishes an inaccurate story). She isn't loyal to society (she allows a miscarriage of justice to go unrequited). She isn't loyal to her staff (she asks them to betray their best journalistic instincts). In fact, she isn't loyal to anything that is noble or life-affirming or that is capable of inspiring a similar loyalty in others.

Clark expects Hackett to behave as a loyal employee and strictly obey her orders. But he has a deeper understanding of what it means to be loyal. For him, it means educating the public. It means being truthful and independent and fair. It means fulfilling the democratic ideals embodied in the motto of the *Sun*: "It Shines for All."

We can now say with some assurance that Hackett makes the right decision about the arrest story, or at least a better decision than Clark does. He may not actually use the Potter Box, but as our analysis shows, his values, principles, and loyalties end up being consistent with each other and the facts. Of course, Hackett is lucky to reach a morally justifiable decision without engaging in systematic reasoning. Those of us who aren't so lucky still need to think ahead.

OUT OF THE BOX

Aristotle notes that just as "one swallow does not make a spring, nor does one sunny day," so acting as you should on one occasion, or even several, doesn't make you a moral person. Hackett is a case in point. Although he acts ethically in relation to the arrest story, he displays a certain lack of character in other situations throughout the film. For example:

1. He neglects his pregnant wife, ignoring her anxieties about impending motherhood, and rejecting her pleas that he take a nine-to-five job and lead a more normal life. "Aspects of good character," philosopher Joel J. Kupperman states, "include appropriate concerns and commitments." Are Hackett's concerns and commitments appropriate? Or does he put too much emphasis on work and not enough on family? Editor Bernie White never develops the proper balance between his personal and professional lives. Now afflicted with two former wives, a daughter who doesn't speak to him, and prostate cancer, he is a lonely old man. Hackett risks following in White's unhappy footsteps.

2. While at the *Sentinel* for a job interview, Hackett is overcome by feelings of journalistic rivalry and steals a story off the editor's desk. "You are the most unethical, unprincipled—" the editor (Spalding Gray) splutters when he finds out. "I can't believe you had the balls to do it!" His outrage may well be justified, though the film treats the incident comically, implying that the editor is perhaps somehow worse than Hackett for wearing a bow tie and suspenders and having a supercilious manner.

3. Hackett allows McDougal, who is angry about some parking tickets he got, to use the paper to conduct a vendetta against the traffic commissioner. Unlike the effort to clear the names of the two black youths, this crusade is a pseudoevent, designed to whip up the mob, not to correct a genuine injustice. At best, it represents typical tabloid sensationalism; at worst, a vindictive exercise of press power.

Seen within the context of the entire film, Hackett appears just as capable as Clark of being unethical, of choosing the wrong means or pursuing the wrong end. His usual pattern of thought and action—what Kupperman would call his "character"—reveals a pronounced tendency to do what is expedient instead of what is right. No wonder almost everyone who knows him is puzzled by his fanatical opposition to the "GOTCHA!" headline. Lying, stealing, and cheating seem much more his characteristic style than does coming to the rescue of others.

Kupperman, an admirer of Aristotle's *Nicomachean Ethics*, writes that "Reliably good moral choice also requires good character." Aristotle believed that as a person is, so a person does, meaning, Roger J. Sullivan explains in *Morality and the Good Life: A Commentary on Aristotle's* Nicomachean Ethics, that "a person will not perform the right kind of actions consistently and for the right reason if he does not have the kind of character which leads him to cherish acting rightly."

The best guarantee of ethical journalism isn't the Potter Box or similar aids to ethical reflection; it is good character, the habitual disposition to seek what a person ought to seek—wisdom, justice, the happiness of others. In *The Journalist in Plato's Cave*, Jay Newman remarks that "journalistic integrity is often simply a matter of habitually applying general principles of justice and morality to all of one's activities as a journalist. A journalist who is a good person," he adds, "is not necessarily a good journalist, but he is almost always a person who carries out his journalistic work with something that deserves to be characterized as journalistic integrity." For such a one, right action would be spontaneous, an ingrained habit of heart and mind, not the agonizing, ad hoc, case-by-case process most of us now undergo.

Contemporary ethicists generally agree that character can't be taught. "There is a contradiction in terms," Kupperman says, "in the idea of a teacher, or anyone else, pressuring or instructing someone to have a strong character." He argues that once beyond the "dogmatic instruction of central moral norms" given to small children— for example, that murder and theft are wrong—teachers and authors shouldn't dictate answers, but outline possible options and stimulate thought. The whole point of moral education is to get people to think for themselves about moral issues. Only then can character development occur.

Here is where the Potter Box ceases to be an academic exercise. As a justification model, it requires us to ask whether the action we contemplate taking is grounded in a consistent and personally meaningful set of values, principles, and loyalties. When Dyck describes the reason for studying ethics, he might as well be describing the utility of the Potter Box itself: "[A] modest but important means by which people can discover, before they act, how they would best like to act, and imaginatively test in advance some of the difficult choices that lie ahead." This kind of testing strengthens empathy and critical thinking and helps us develop good habits of choice, the very essence of character.

Journalists face tough ethical choices every day on the street and in the newsroom. *The Paper* is a realistic film in that it shows journalists being forced under deadline pressure to choose from several murky options. How do you make the best choice? The recommendations of ethicists can be summed up in a few simple guidelines: take your time; avoid thinking in clichés like "freedom of the press" or "the public's right to know"; consider the happiness of others; and, in dark moments, follow the sun.

QUESTIONS TO CONSIDER

1. Do tabloids have less duty to the truth than do broadsheets? Does duty to the truth vary across the media? Refer in your answer to print, radio, television, film, and the Internet.

2. What are the traits of a moral person? Of a moral journalist? Is it possible to be an immoral person, but a moral journalist, or vice versa? What does *The Paper* suggest?

3. Is Hackett's theft of the story from the *Sentinel* justified? Apply the Potter Box to the situation.

4. What is the ideal balance between work and family? Do any of the main characters in *The Paper*—Hackett, Clark, or White— achieve it? Are media corporations ethically responsible for helping employees develop in their lives what Kupperman calls "appropriate concerns and commitments"?

5. Adler states that "[m]oney is wrongly desired when it is desired as an end itself and not purely as a means." In *The Paper*, which characters desire money as an end itself and which as a means? Give examples, either historical or hypothetical, of money being desired by the media as a means to a good end.

6. What is more important for a journalist to possess, character or talent? Why?

FURTHER READING

Adler, Mortimer J. *Desires Right and Wrong: The Ethics of Enough*. New York: Macmillan, 1991.

Bok, Sissela. *Lying: Moral Choice in Public and Private Life*. New York: Pantheon, 1978.

Christians, Clifford G., Kim B. Rotzoll, and Mark Fackler. *Media Ethics: Cases and Moral Reasoning*. 4th ed. New York: Longman, 1995.

Dyck, Arthur C. *On Human Care*. Nashville, Tenn.: Abingdon, 1977.

Krajicek, David J. *Scooped! Media Miss Real Story on Crime While Chasing Sex, Sleaze, and Celebrities*. New York: Columbia University Press, 1998.

Kupperman, Joel J. *Character*. New York: Oxford University Press, 1991.

Newman, Jay. *The Journalist in Plato's Cave*. Rutherford, N.J.: Farleigh Dickinson University Press, 1989.

Patterson, Philip, and Lee Wilkins, eds. *Media Ethics: Issues and Cases*. 3rd ed. Boston: McGraw-Hill, 1998.

Sullivan, Roger J. *Morality and the Good Life: A Commentary on Aristotle's Nicomachean Ethics*. Memphis, Tenn.: Memphis State University Press, 1977.

6

12 Angry Men: Appeal to Reason

If you are ever arrested, you can thank Nicolaus Copernicus, Isaac Newton, and Galileo Galilei—among others—that you will face a jury of your peers rather than an inquisition. Trial by jury is so commonplace and pervasive (courtroom dramas never go out of style in newspapers, films, and television shows) that it seems unexceptional. The idea that ordinary, untrained citizens can be trusted to pass judgment on their peers, however, was an extraordinary step in the development of civic freedom.

The notion that individuals are autonomous and rational springs from the scientific revolution of the Enlightenment. Scientists like Galileo and Newton overturned religious explanations of the origin and functioning of nature and in so doing elevated fact and observation over belief. They produced a new vision of the universe as an ordered and predictable "world-machine" set into motion by the hand of a Creator and working in perfect balance and harmony. Several of the founding fathers were adherents of Deism, a religious philosophy compatible with their scientific worldview, which proposed that God designed the universe and withdrew to let it function as it would—a sort of celestial absentee landlord.

Enlightenment philosophers reasoned that if the world had merely been set in motion by a supreme being and operated according to discoverable principles, no person could claim to be divinely endowed with moral superiority. And if *that* was true, then all people must enter into nature in a state of equality, each endowed with the power to reason and the right to determine his or her own fate. These are fundamental premises of democracy.

If reason allowed humans to fathom the stars, surely it empowered them to understand and manage their societies. The Enlightenment taught Western man to steer his course by the facts, not the heavens. Philosophers such as John Locke, Thomas Hobbes, Charles Montesquieu, and René Descartes argued that because human beings are endowed with reason, they could investigate and discover the physical and metaphysical truths of their world. "Knowledge was not imprinted, once and for all, on man's brain by God; it was to be discovered, by experience in the world," Locke declared. Enlightenment philosophers imagined new social orders that reflected new scientific truths and they translated Newtonian physics into metaphysics by taking principles of physical science and applying them to the human condition.

The physical and metaphysical principles posited by Enlightenment thinkers is reflected in the founding documents of the United States. The founders were children of the Enlightenment, practical philosophers constructing a science of statehood as they went along. Indeed, they referred to the task of creating the new nation as a "great experiment." The tripartite architecture of the federal government, with legislative, executive, and judicial branches serving to check and balance each other, is a manifestation of Newton's world-machine.

DELIBERATE STRANGERS

A discussion of such lofty philosophies may seem far afield from a film about twelve angry men deciding the fate of a boy accused of murder in a cramped Manhattan jury room. In fact, the courtroom is an ideal expression of the belief that human beings, by relying on observation and intellect, can manage the affairs of their communities. Rights of due process and free speech spring from the same philosophical root. Because people have the power to reason, they have the right to be heard and to consider evidence in legal matters involving their peers. Journalists also use reason to construct narratives that assign meaning to events in society. Those who would do so have an ethical obligation to use their full intellectual faculties to search for truth.

12 Angry Men, produced in 1957 and again in 1998 (this chapter is based on the original production), was written by Reginald Rose during the height of McCarthyism, a period when basic liberties and long-held rules of due process were trampled by communist witch-hunters. Anticommunists unethically twisted allegations into "evidence," hid facts inconvenient to their cause, and degraded the idea of due process by conducting rigged show trials.

12 Angry Men's characters comprise a cross-section of American archetypes who are thrown together to decide the fate of a teenaged boy accused of murdering his father after an argument. The evidence against the boy seems overwhelming, but concrete facts are transformed into shadows as jurors deliberate over the boy's guilt. The film makes clear that the mechanism of the law is meaningless unless individuals take responsibility for their roles in the execution of justice.

While the fate of the boy is central to the drama, what is really on trial in *12 Angry Men* is our assumption that citizens possess the intellect, dispassion, discipline, and sense of duty to exercise the rights and responsibility of citizenship. In the end, reason triumphs, the boy is saved, and democratic ideals are affirmed. But the journey to affirmation raises many troubling questions about our capacity to live up to the expectations of our political philosophy.

I WITNESS NEWS?

The courtroom drama of *12 Angry Men* serves multiple purposes in the exploration of media ethics. In sifting facts and reaching judgments, jurors call on the same kind of reasoning reporters and news consumers use to make sense of the world. Each considers evidence in an attempt to discern the most plausible explanation for an event. The notion is simple: Once the facts are known, truth can be discovered. What seemed certain to Enlightenment philosophers, however, becomes elusive when taken from the rarefied plane of pure ideas and put to work in the real world. The concept of "evidence" is an amorphous one. What constitutes a "fact"? How can we know that reasoning has been used properly to connect these facts into a broader context that justifies our conclusions and subsequent actions? The judge's charge to the jurors in *12 Angry Men* who will decide whether a fellow citizen lives or dies—"to sit down and try to separate the facts from the fancy"—is deceptively simple.

The film reveals the difficulty citizens face in trying to separate prejudices and perceptions from physical facts. It also honors the inherent beauty of sweet reason. *12 Angry Men* is not, per se, about journalism, but it does call into question the fundamental processes—personal, psychological, professional, and moral—that guide journalists as they prepare a daily report of happenings in the world.

The U.S. Constitution asserts that "all men are created equal," but they don't all end up that way. Juror #8 (Henry Fonda) is dressed in an angelic white suit and certainly embodies our best possibilities, but other jurors lack either his intellect or sense of empathy, or both. Juror #7 (Jack Warden) is itching to get to a baseball game. He is willing to vote whichever way will get him to the ballpark on time. He has no sense of duty. Juror #10 (Ed Begley) is a bigot, who sees the trial of the boy as a way to vindicate his racist views. Juror #3 (Lee J. Cobb) has a personal score to settle; to him, the boy is a living reminder of a son who has defied and abandoned him. Furious as other jurors begin to doubt the boy's guilt, he declares, "We're trying to put a guilty man in the chair where he belongs!"—a fundamental misunderstanding of a jury's duty, to say the least. Juror #12 (Robert Webber), an advertising man, has been trained to reduce ideas to slogans.

As the deliberations begin, all of the jurors are ready to convict with the exception of Juror #8. This juror best illustrates the Enlightenment concept that the duty of the learned person is not to make unfounded assertions, but to ask questions. Shouted down over and over again by his peers as they reject his alternative explanations of the murder, he keeps replying, "But it's *possible*." He understands that "facts" do not speak for themselves. Asked by Juror #3 if he really believes the boy is innocent, #8 replies like any good scientist confronted with a puzzling phenomenon: "I don't know." Pressed to defend his defiant vote, he explains, "There were eleven votes for guilty. It's not easy to raise my hand and send a boy to die without talking about it first."

At different times in the reporting process, a journalist functions as judge, jury, prosecution, and defense. It is beyond the purview of reporters to independently declare the subjects of news stories to be guilty or innocent, but they do decide what stories are worthy of coverage, what facts are worthy of printing, and what sources are worthy of quotation. Once reporters make their determinations, they submit their findings to the court of public opinion in the form of a news story. Public deliberation then becomes the grist for yet more narratives.

By deeming an event to be newsworthy, or a source to be credible, journalists can elevate raw perceptions into facts, as sociologist Gaye Tuchman points out: "Clearly, the language of news prose contains a special relationship to the everyday world, for, like any language, it both frames and accomplishes discourse. It is perception and it guides perception; it reconstitutes the everyday world."

The news stories journalists write, based on what they consider to be credible evidence, have manifold effects:

- They shape, for better or worse, public perceptions of community members who find themselves—perhaps for the first and only time in their lives—in the cross-hairs of public scrutiny. Stories create labels; they can burden an innocent with the stain of guilt and bequeath to a scoundrel the aura of sainthood.

- Sometimes the extralegal power of news organizations is so great that it can sway potential jurors, leading judges to order trials moved far away to avoid seating jurors biased by news accounts.

- Citizens base personal, political, and economic judgments, in large part, on information they read in the newspaper. They also have to live with the long-term effects of public policies. Many cities are stuck with white elephant civic projects that at their inception were touted as tonics because the "evidence" of their utility was provided by public officials and news outlets.

- News accounts give to us an image of the wider world beyond our physical reach. The shape of the news report can cause citizens to feel undue fear or optimism about the outside world. Researcher George Gerbner convincingly argues that pervasive television violence, for instance, is "politically exploitable" because viewers mistake the media world for the real world and demand greater protection from authorities, often at the expense of their civil liberties.

A STREAM OF PERCEPTIONS

Reporters are expected, but not necessarily trained, to observe. Much of what they report, however, is based on the accounts of others, most of whom also are not trained observers. Journalists rarely witness a plane crash, a murder, or an act of terrorism; instead, they rush to the scene afterward to interview people who were at the scene and saw what happened—or at least claim to have seen what happened. How reliable are these observers? What forces shape their perceptions? What constitutes a journalistic fact—that is, a statement that can appear without being preceded by the word "allegedly" or followed by attribution? Given that the perceptions of diverse witnesses or commentators are bound to vary, how does a reporter reconcile conflicting accounts to produce a coherent narrative?

It is important to remember that just as news sources try to "spin" the facts to sway reporters and readers to their positions, jurors at a trial are not presented merely with raw evidence. The ultimate objective of defenders and prosecutors is to convince a jury that the evidence means what they say it means. In the popular imagination, the highlights of a trial are the opening and closing statements, which are nuanced, sophisticated, and purposeful narratives.

Journalists and their sources are individuals with free will and rational intellects (at least most of the time, we hope), but they are also products of their times, their cultures, their upbringings and experiences, and the ideologies that drive the societies in which they live. As Karl Marx observed: "Men make their own history, but they do not make it as they please; they do not make it under self-selected circumstances, but under circumstances existing already, given and transmitted from the past. The tradition of all dead generations weighs like an Alp on the brains of the living."

As news reporters or news consumers, we do not approach each new story or event afresh, but instead interpret it through the perceptual filters we bring to it. As journalist and philosopher Walter Lippmann explained, "A report is always the joint product of the knower and the known, in which the role of observer is always selective and usually creative." Numerous studies in the social sciences, for instance, have shown that a white person brought up in an atmosphere of racial prejudice who has not had significant dealings with African Americans is likely to feel fear or disdain—or both— when an African American approaches him on the street. Such prejudices have shaped common police methods such as "profiling" —which leads police to pull over African American motorists simply because they are dark skinned. In other words, jurors, reporters, and readers are conditioned to see what they expect to see.

One way to visualize these forces of identity is by using a model we call "The Stream of Perceptions" (see fig. 6.1). The "Stream of

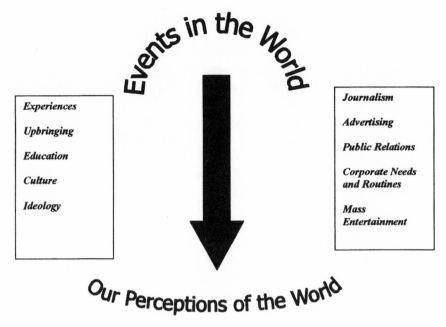

Figure 6.1   The Stream of Perceptions

Perceptions" is a simple visual model that depicts the complex and often disorienting sources of our ideas about events and phenomena in the world beyond our senses. A person is born with innate traits and distinct characteristics; he or she is no mere lump of clay to be wholly shaped by the world. But shape us the world does. Lippmann pointed out the inherent difficulties of conveying "reality" in a news account. There is "a world outside," he wrote, and then there are "pictures in our head" of that world. Those two worlds are often at odds. Events outside of our personal experience are necessarily constructed from news accounts, stories, books, movies, and our own established attitudes about the world and the people in it.

News of the world comes to us in a stream whose composition is transformed as numerous tributaries empty into it. Just as a sample taken from the headwaters of the Mississippi River would not have the same chemical composition as a sample taken from its mouth in the Gulf of Mexico, so events are transformed each time they are reshaped into a different symbolic context. Each of the jurors in *12 Angry Men* brings a distinct set of experiences and preconceptions to the task of deciding the guilt of a boy charged with murder. Even though the jurors don't even learn each others' names during the course of the tumultuous deliberations, they reveal much about the sources of their perceptions, assumptions, and prejudices.

One juror's slum upbringing, for instance, will allow him to discredit a key piece of evidence. Another juror's age and experience will allow him to provide special insight into the motives of some of the witnesses. Exposure to stereotypes in the media has shaped some jurors' perceptions of the accused and the victim. Some of the jurors have definite ideas about the neighborhood where the crime was committed and the nature of the people who live there, even though it is unlikely few have been in that neighborhood or know its ethnic residents. These perceptions and assumptions coalesced at the confluence of cultural learning, personal experience, and, likely, exposure to the media.

The film draws the viewer into the jury's debate by deliberately omitting the trial itself. What viewers learn about the case, they learn through the perceptual filters of the jurors. And, by the end, it is clear that "hard evidence" can be illusory. Without the benefit of hearing the actual testimony, we are left to fathom the evidence as it is recounted and interpreted, often inaccurately, by the jurors. In this way, the film vividly evokes the journalistic method. Reporters, too, piece together accounts from sources who saw or heard about or offered explanations for events. Much of what appears in a news story would be dismissed by a court as hearsay evidence.

The oppressive presence of the clock hangs heavy over the cinematic drama just as it does over the real-life drama of newsgathering. Juries are not under a precise deadline, but a jury that cannot reach a decision within a reasonable amount of time is declared deadlocked. Additionally, if new evidence is discovered after the conclusion of a trial that has ended in acquittal, the double-jeopardy clause forbids retrying the case. In a newsroom, deliberations over the justice of a story end when the presses roll. Like reporters, who are often juggling several stories at once, distractions eat at most of the jurors in *12 Angry Men*. Many would rather be somewhere else and pressure the others to reach a verdict quickly.

PRIDE AND PREJUDICE

Many of the arguments made by the jurors in *12 Angry Men* are not aimed at fashioning a reasoned interpretation of the evidence.

Instead, they use the deliberations as a forum to assert the validity of their beliefs. The objective of some jurors is to win a competition by proving their beliefs about the world are correct.

Personalizing the debate is antithetical to the jury's charge, which is to impartially examine and weigh evidence; in the end, jurors are expected to decide whether the defendant is guilty beyond a reasonable doubt or acquit him—which is not necessarily a declaration of innocence. Juror #10, exasperated as votes turn toward acquittal, laments, "We're letting him slip through our fingers!"

Juror #11 (George Voskovec), a quiet immigrant, is not immediately swayed to Juror #8's views of the case, but he is increasingly influenced by his spirit of inquiry. When he is chastised by the bullying Juror #3 for being disloyal to the group that wants to convict, he replies, "I don't believe I have to be loyal to one side or the other. I'm just asking."

Juror #10 clearly sees the case as an opportunity to validate his bigoted views. Selectively citing evidence, #10 makes offers circular illogic in an attempt to convince his peers that the young defendant must be a murderer because, in his worldview, boys like him are necessarily killers: "We heard the facts, didn't we?" he bellows. "You're not going to tell me we're supposed to believe this kid knowing what he is. Look . . . I've lived among them all my life. You can't believe a word they say, you know that. I mean, they're born liars."

While a lifetime in the presence of "the other" has only inflamed the prejudice of Juror #10, it is worth pointing out that modern reporters often have little or no firsthand experience in the worlds of many of those they write about. While crime stories, especially, originate in poor or minority neighborhoods, the typical reporter today is white, has a middle-class background, has attended college, and is likely to live in the suburbs. Most reporters have had little exposure to some of the groups of people they "reconstruct" for public consumption.

Juror #5 (Jack Klugman), however, has a strong sense of empathy with the accused. Even though #5 is convinced through most of the deliberations that the boy is guilty, his understanding of the defendant's world gives him special insight into the circumstances surrounding the murder. He, too, emerged from the world of noise, sweat, and squalor that produced the boy, and that experience enables him to refute a key piece of evidence—the knife thrust that produced the fatal wound. Unlike the others on the jury, including the erudite Juror #8 and the sophisticated Juror #4 (E. G. Marshall), Juror #5 has witnessed several knife fights. As the evidence is resifted, it dawns on him that the version of the knife attack presented by the prosecution doesn't make sense.

"Wait a minute. What's the matter with me?" #5 declares in a moment of memory and revelation. "Give me that," he says, taking the knife. Asked if he has ever witnessed a knife fight, he replies, "In my backyard. On the stoop. In the vacant lot across the street. Too many of them. Switch-knives came with the neighborhood where I lived. Funny, I didn't think of it before. I guess you try to forget those things." Flicking the knife open, he demonstrates how it is meant to be used. "Anyone who's ever used a switch-knife would never have stabbed downward. You don't handle a switch-knife that way. You use it underhand."

A journalist covering the story of the murder would probably not question a police report that contained such an obvious error—those aren't the kinds of things they teach in journalism schools. Without the inclusion of Juror #5, the jury would have been denied an important perspective. How many perspectives are missing in the media because the alternative viewpoints and experiences of minorities are not available in the news report?

BAGGAGE HANDLERS

Ethnic prejudice is at the heart of *12 Angry Men*, but to leave it at that would be to oversimplify the personal, social, and political dynamics portrayed in the film. More than prejudice drives the attitudes of the jurors toward the young man accused of killing his father.

Smoldering with anger and bitterness, Juror #3 brings intense personal biases to the table. The strict and brutal upbringing he gave his son alienated the boy, whom he has not seen since an argument that ended with the boy punching him. He strongly identifies with the murdered father. A psychological phenomenon known as "transference" posits that when we encounter a situation that is similar to one we have encountered in the past, we "transfer" the feelings and perceptions we associate with that initial experience. Those transferred feelings then shape our perception of the new experience. For Juror #3, the alleged patricide at the center of the trial is a near-replay of his experiences with his own son and he is the last to be swayed by the evidence that casts reasonable doubt on the defendant's guilt. "Damned kids, you work and slave. . . . If you ask me, I'd slap those tough kids before they start—it'd save us a lot of time and money."

Juror #8 is the drama's catalyst. An architect by trade, he is accustomed to precision and cold analysis of the facts. But he is also empathetic. "I kept putting myself in the kid's place," he says. "Look, this kid's been kicked around all his life. He's a wild, angry kid and that's all he's ever been. And why? Because he's been hit on the head once a day every day." #8 also points out that the boy's defense was inadequate and that his court-appointed attorney did little to challenge the prosecution's evidence—that is why the jury must do so now.

Jurors #3, #8, and #10 dominate the deliberations and present three distinct points of view to their fellow jurors, who are essentially followers in the drama. Despite their fervor, Jurors #3 and #10 are not driven merely by emotion or unreason in their quest to convict. Detestable as they seem, each draws on the evidence to shape his argument. "These are facts," Juror #3 declares. "It's obvious you can't refute facts." Indeed, the facts are damning to the accused:

- A neighbor heard the boy vow to kill his father, then sounds of a scuffle. Shortly afterwards, he saw the boy rush down the hall in a panic.
- The boy had been seen with a knife identical to the murder weapon.
- The boy cannot account for his whereabouts during the crime. His alibi, that he was at the movies, is undercut by the fact that he cannot name the film he saw. In addition, no one at the movie theater remembered seeing him there.
- Most damning, a woman who lived across the elevated train track awoke during the night and, through the windows of the passing train, watched the boy stab his father.

Given the evidence, the impatience of most of the jurors to vote guilty and be done with it—virtually ensuring that the boy will be executed—seems justified. Juror #8 cannot directly refute any of the evidence at the outset of the deliberations, but is haunted by the knowledge that if the jury is wrong, an innocent boy will die. If that happens, not incidentally, a killer will also escape justice. #8 does not argue that the boy is innocent, only that it would be irresponsible and immoral to send him to die without examining the facts. Lazy reporters who only superficially inquire into stories that will affect individuals and communities are guilty of the same kind of moral lapse as jurors who fail to weigh, analyze, and question evidence and testimony.

CUTS LIKE A KNIFE

The task of sifting and scrutinizing facts is complex. Not only must the validity and source of each fact be examined, but also the facts must all be fitted together into a coherent whole. Each fact must be questioned. The murder weapon is an excellent example. The boy claims he found the switchblade knife that the prosecution has argued was the murder weapon. During the trial, the knife was introduced into a narrow contextual frame that drives the jurors' debate. The premise of that frame is that the knife is unusual and clearly made the wound that killed the boy's father.

Juror #8, like a good journalist, reaches outside this convenient frame. During a break in deliberations, he easily finds a knife that is identical to the murder weapon. Dramatically jabbing the identical knife into the jury room table, he destroys the premise that underlies the knife's damning value as evidence. The knife is *not* unusual— a revelation that weakens the underlying assumption that since the man was killed with such a knife and the boy had such a knife, the boy must be the killer. Juror #8 provides a new context for the knife and uses it, by implication, to call into doubt all of the other "airtight" evidence on which his fellow jurors have decided the boy is guilty and therefore deserving of hasty justice.

Once the evidence of the murder weapon is called into question, other evidence begins to crumble. If the knife evidence is illusory, what other "facts" might be flawed? Reason begets reason and gradually other jurors are roused from their complacency by plausible, alternative explanations for facts presented at trial. For instance, a downstairs neighbor heard the boy argue with his father and then heard a loud thud, presumably caused by a body hitting the floor. Seconds later, the neighbor, an old man, opened his door to see the boy rush past. Taken individually, the facts seem to leave little doubt that the boy killed his father and dashed from the crime scene. When

Juror #8 suggests that the jurors "take two pieces of evidence and put them together," however, this conclusion begins to crumble.

Aged Juror #9 (Joseph Sweeney), drawing on his unique perspective, employs empathy to help Juror #8 defuse the old man's testimony. He notes that the old man had come to court dressed in his best, albeit shabby, suit. He explains that many people pass through the river of life without making so much as a ripple; the insignificance of their passage is magnified as death draws near. Any reporter who's covered a crime story will attest that very often the most willing "witness" at the scene is the person who didn't see anything. Having one's name in the paper confers a certain status.

"I think I know this man better than anyone," Juror #9 says. "This is a quiet, frightened, insignificant man who has been nothing all his life, who's never had recognition or his name in any newspapers. A man like this needs to be listened to, to be quoted just once. No, he wouldn't really lie, but perhaps he made himself believe he heard those words and recognized the boy's face."

The man's apparent eagerness for public notice does not mean, in and of itself, that his testimony is untrue. But it does lead to other questions, questions outside of the frame presented during the trial. Juror #8 shows that given the dimensions of the man's apartment, it is unlikely that he could have gotten to his door within fifteen seconds, as he claimed he did, to see the boy rush past. Acting out the lame old man's testimony, Juror #8 shows that even at a rapid pace, he could not have reached the door in less than forty-one seconds. (The reenactment scene mischievously demonstrates the elusiveness of facts: time the scene and you will note that it actually takes #8 only thirty seconds to reach the hypothetical door in the jury room.) Juror #3, desperate to punish the boy, again dismisses evidence that undermines his cause. He argues, paradoxically, "He was an old man, half the time he was confused. How can he be positive about anything?"

As the floodgates of skepticism open wider, troubling questions about the evidence stream forth. Why would a killer wipe his fingerprints from a knife and then leave it at the crime scene? Why would he return later knowing the police would be waiting? How could a man hear the thud of a body while at the same time a woman sees the murder through the windows of the screaming elevated train that ran past both their windows? He could not, of course—the train would have drowned out noise from the murder scene. But even after Juror #8 dispels or casts into doubt much of the evidence, the woman's testimony remains. A light sleeper, she awoke, looked out her window, and, through the windows of the empty train, saw the boy kill his father. Such a view through a moving train is possible. Juror #8's antagonists challenge him to explain away her testimony. She had no reason to lie.

By this point in the drama, it has become clear that only by approaching facts critically and looking beyond their surface can one refute or affirm them. Caught up in the spirit of Juror #8's critical inquiry, elderly Juror #9 again wonders whether a combination of human vanity, psychological expectations, and misperception might have combined to produce an illusion instead of a fact. Noticing Juror #4, who has approached the evidence analytically and does not possess a reasonable doubt about the boy's guilt, rubbing his eyes, Juror #9 is startled into reexamining a fragment of memory he had dismissed as inconsequential during the trial.

He notices that Juror #4's glasses have left an impression on the bridge of his nose. The witness, he recalls, had a similar impression on her nose. Unless she slept with her glasses on, her story that she awoke and happened to look out the window at the moment the killing occurred is not plausible.

OBJECTION

For much of the twentieth century, journalists have been urged to be "objective." As it is popularly—and incorrectly—defined, objectivity has come to mean keeping one's opinion out of the story and offering facts without comment.

Lippmann, fearful of the power of propaganda and the enormous power of unscrupulous publishers to mold public perceptions, proposed that journalism strive for professionalism and scientific dispassion. In Lippmann's original conception of objectivity, reporters would be trained observers, free of partisan and corporate biases, who would rationally evaluate and interpret events.

Lippmann's vision quickly devolved into the idea that reporters should merely discover and present "facts," without interpretation, leaving readers to figure out their meaning. This diluted objectivity was the antithesis of Lippmann's ideal and led to a kind of journalistic relativism in which assertions about the world (made mostly by authority figures) are simply passed along as facts in news reports.

If spokespeople for all mainstream viewpoints are presented, "balance" is achieved.

This *Cliff's Notes* objectivity assumes that facts are tangible things that speak for themselves. It also assumes that all statements are relatively equal if made by recognized news sources, such as government officials, corporate executives, and scientists. If a Democrat says the sky is green, the modern reporter knows that a story must also include a Republican's assertion that the sky is green. It's not the reporter's job to look up and see for him- or herself. Similarly, the jurors in *12 Angry Men* believe that it is not their duty to critically examine arguments and evidence, only to consider them at face value.

Juror #8 may not be a reporter, but his methods of encountering and making sense of events are instructive to aspiring journalists. He employs critical intelligence and reason and is open to the perspectives and insights of others whose experiences are different from his own. Journalists too often rely on the "usual suspects" to provide the raw fodder for news stories. City hall possesses politically sanctioned authority and routinely furnishes information to reporters. As a result, reporters often simply process and pass along the information city hall provides without much scrutiny or critical analysis. What if it's wrong—by happenstance or design?

Deadlines and production schedules make it impractical for reporters to roam the world looking for significant stories. Working hand-in-glove with established sources makes the news world-machine manageable and serves the interests of both reporters and sources. As Michael Schudson observes, "News gathering is normally a matter of the representatives of one bureaucracy picking up prefabricated news items from representatives of another bureaucracy." The problem with this is that information packaged by city hall or other authority agencies arrives in a package aimed at accomplishing city hall's objectives, just as prosecutors employ and interpret evidence selectively to gain a conviction.

Publishers embraced diluted objectivity in part because it allowed them to maintain control of the news columns. A reporter, ideally, is charged with discovering the truth, but in reality reporters work for organizations with ideological, political, and economic interests. Some facts—such as partnerships with financial institutions that would raise conflict-of-interest concerns or environmental problems at the newspaper plant—are inconvenient to news organizations. That is why it is the prerogative of a news organization's management to interpret the facts on the editorial page. Reporters provide the stories, but the publisher constructs the reality.

Juror #6 (Ed Binns), a laborer who is used to taking orders, illustrates the journalist's dilemma. Convinced that the facts must be true because the prosecutor said they are, he asks Juror #8 why he insists on looking deeper. "Suppose you were the one on trial?" Juror #8 asks. Juror #6 replies: "I'm not used to supposin'. I'm just a working man. My boss does the supposin'."

In a technical sense, a jury is subordinate to the judge. But in a larger sense, the jury is at the heart of a trial. Jurors decide guilt or innocence and therefore have a duty to engage in a vigorous analysis of the case. Reporters, like jurors, should adhere to the judge's dictum to "separate the facts from the fancy," but are often prevented from doing so by their version of "objectivity" and their reliance on convenient, but limiting, official sources.

RESETTING THE CLOCKWORK UNIVERSE

The physical "facts" on which our political system is based have been largely discredited. Quantum physics and Chaos Theory have shattered Newton's clockwork blueprint of the universe. That does not mean, however, the philosophical and political principles derived from Enlightenment science are unworthy or unworkable. Reason may or may not be a gift, but it certainly is not a given; it arises from hard intellectual work, a willingness to extend empathy, and a commitment to justice. In the end, the legacy of the Enlightenment philosophers is not their answers, but their questions—and the spirit of patient, critical inquiry that, ironically, ultimately led to the demise of the physical worldview on which they based their conclusions.

Can twelve average citizens come together and, through the exercise of reason, discover the truth about a crime? Can news reporters really "piece together" the disparate perceptions that coalesce around a news event to produce a narrative that has the ring of truth? Enlightenment science said they could. Quantum physics has not yet proposed an answer. Perhaps as citizens, media workers, and media consumers we had best keep trying.

QUESTIONS TO CONSIDER

1. How do you know what you know? Choose a city or country you've never visited and describe it in one hundred words. If

you've never been there, how did you come to "know" what you described? What forces formed your perceptions? Do a little research; do the "facts" you've described match the facts about the place you find in encyclopedias or reference books?

2. Think back to the evidence as it was presented in the film. At the onset of the deliberations, the evidence appears to be overwhelming. At what point might you have a developed a "reasonable doubt" about the boy's guilt? What questions might you have asked at various points in the deliberations?

3. Choose a news story from today's paper that describes an event, such as an accident, a crime, or a battle. How did the reporter choose the sources for the article? To what extent do you think the article faithfully depicts the reality of what happened? What frames the narrative—that is, why did the reporter consider certain facts to be worth reporting and what might be left outside the frame? What questions would you have asked and tried to answer if you covered the story? Do the accounts of the sources in the article add up? Are their statements based on direct observation or are they secondhand?

4. Break into groups. Discuss a controversial question, such as "Is the death penalty justified?" or "Is abortion legally and morally justified?" Is it difficult to confine the argument to principles of reason, or do the emotions of group members overwhelm the discussion? Rather than try to definitively answer the question, let everyone state his or her position and then try to examine what forces—culture, religion, experiences, and media exposure—might have contributed to each person's position.

5. Would you trust a group of your peers to decide your fate if you were on trial? Would the race, gender, ethnic background, or economic class of the jurors make a difference to you?

FURTHER READING

Bronowski, J., and Bruce Mazlish. *The Western Intellectual Tradition, from Leonardo to Hegel.* New York: Harper, 1960.

Gerbner, George. *Violence and Terror in the Mass Media.* Lanham, Md.: UNIPUB, 1988.

Lippmann, Walter. *Public Opinion.* New York: Macmillan, 1960.

Marx, Karl. *The Eighteenth Brumaire of Louis Bonaparte.* New York: International, 1964.

Schudson, Michael. "Deadlines, Datelines and History." In *Reading the News*, ed. Robert Karl Manoff and Michael Schudson. New York: Pantheon, 1986.

Tuchman, Gaye. *Making News: A Study in the Construction of Reality*. New York: The Free Press, 1978.

7

Eight Men Out:
A Double Play in Ethics

Eight Men Out, a film about the most famous scandal in baseball history, the throwing of the 1919 World Series, turns a kind of cinematic double play, raising a host of ethical questions also pertinent to journalists. The baseball field may seem far removed from the field of journalism, but some revealing analogies can be drawn between the two. Both baseball players and journalists perform for audiences; both operate within an elaborate system of rules, ideals, and habits that have grown up over time and become hallowed by usage; and both work for business owners whose interests don't necessarily coincide with theirs.

The actual facts of the "Black Sox" scandal, as the World Series fix came to be called, have always been in dispute—from which players took money to how much each received. Eight White Sox were indicted in 1920 for conspiring with gamblers to throw the series against the Cincinnati Reds. Although acquitted of criminal charges the next year, they were banned from professional baseball for life by the game's first commissioner, Judge Kenesaw Mountain Landis. The players included the great "Shoeless" Joe Jackson, who hit .375 in the series and whose career batting average of .356 is still the third highest of all time. The others were first baseman Arnold "Chick" Gandil, shortstop Charles "Swede" Risberg, third baseman Buck

Weaver, utility infielder Fred McMullen, outfielder Oscar "Happy" Felsch, and pitchers Eddie Cicotte and Claude "Lefty" Williams. Eliot Asinof, who wrote the 1963 book on which *Eight Men Out* is based, considered them all "victims," men caught by forces far beyond their understanding or control. "The owners poured out a stream of pious, pompous verbiage about how pure they were," Asinof explains. "The gamblers said nothing, kept themselves hidden, protected themselves. . . . But the ballplayers didn't even know enough to call a lawyer. They only knew how to play baseball."

Whether innocent or guilty, victims or traitors, Jackson and the rest of the Black Sox have earned a permanent place in American popular culture. They have been the subject of novels, poems, songs, and films. Hollywood reimagined the scandal beginning with the 1927 silent comedy *Casey at the Bat* and continuing through the 1958 musical *Damn Yankees* to *The Natural* (1984) and *Field of Dreams* (1989), both of which overlay baseball with a gooey mythopoetic glaze. Only *Eight Men Out* (1988) has attempted anything like a realistic portrayal of the scandal, picturing the decision to participate in the fix as ethically complex, characterized by mixed feelings and unexpected consequences. "*Eight Men Out* certainly is about ethics," says John Sayles, who wrote and directed the film. "Each of the guys who betrays his teammates has a different button that is pushed for him to say, Yes, I'll do it. Even within that, there's the ethics of one guy who knows about it and won't throw the series but also won't rat on his friends."

In this chapter, we will identify some of the ethical issues raised in *Eight Men Out* and discuss how they might apply to journalists. We will examine whether employers and managers have a responsibility to create a work environment in which employees feel valued and are able to flourish. We will reflect on the parallels between baseball players' obligations to fans and journalists' obligations to readers, and ask under what conditions, if any, these can be abrogated or suspended. We will explore whether there are times when refusing to be a team player, "one of the boys," is the right thing to do. We will look at the various roles played by the press in the film—recorder, cheerleader, and investigator—and try to distinguish the ethical from the questionable. We will analyze whether the summary banning of the Black Sox was just; that is, whether baseball (or journalism) can tolerate cheaters in its ranks. Lastly, and notwithstanding what the jaunty ragtime music on the soundtrack seems to imply, we will consider whether it is ever possible to be unethical and happy.

OWNING UP

Many baseball historians blame the Black Sox scandal on the miserly avarice of team owner Charles Comiskey. The argument goes that if Comiskey had paid his players what they were actually worth, they never would have agreed to throw the World Series. Despite the White Sox being one of the most profitable teams in the majors, its payroll was among the lowest. And Comiskey skimped not only on salaries, but also on meal money. He even charged his players for laundering their uniforms. When they protested by wearing the same increasingly dirty uniforms for several weeks, he had the uniforms removed from their lockers and fined the players.

Eight Men Out, which is largely sympathetic to the plight of the Black Sox, recreates examples of Comiskey's tightfistedness. Comiskey (Clifton James) had promised his players a big bonus if they won the American League pennant, but as the audience sees early in the film, the bonus turns out to be a case of flat champagne. Seething with resentment, some of the players become almost eager to sell out. Their corruptibility surprises Joseph "Sport" Sullivan (Kevin Tighe), the gambler to whom first baseman Chick Gandil (Michael Rooker) proposes the fix. "You say you can find seven men on the best team ever to take the field willing to throw the series?" Sullivan asks. "I find that hard to believe." To which Gandil ruefully replies, "You never played for Charlie Comiskey."

What makes Comiskey seem especially vicious is that the players are defenseless against his depredations. Until court rulings in the 1970s, professional baseball players rather resembled indentured servants. Their contracts contained a "reserve clause" that prevented them from shopping around for the best salary after each season. They were bound to their teams from the moment they signed to the day they were released or traded. In the film, Comiskey abuses his position and power as team owner, exploiting his legal hold over his players to the fullest. He acknowledges no obligation, based on either shared humanity or common purpose, to treat them with care, dignity, and respect.

All this has interesting implications for media owners. Investigative reporter Robert Sherrill points out that sending journalists to an ethics boot camp wouldn't necessarily improve journalism. "The reason," he says, "is that most of the really significant crumminess in journalism is not at the bottom but at the very top." Today the vast majority of journalists work for news outlets owned by profit-seeking corporations. While there is nothing inherently wrong with turning a profit, there is something wrong with doing so at the expense of quality journalism. It isn't enough for the news media to be profitable; they must also strive to be socially responsible. That is the least the public should expect in return for allowing the media constitutionally protected privileges.

Media ethics begins, then, not at the level of reporters and editors, but at the higher level of owners and managers, where corporate policies are established, resources are allocated, and annual profit goals are set. "Corporate decisions made hundreds of miles from the newsroom," Gene Goodwin and Ron F. Smith advise in their book *Groping for Ethics in Journalism*, "may have as much to do with how well journalists perform as decisions made in the newsroom." If media owners decide to squeeze out a few extra bucks by overworking the news staff or by reducing the size of the news hole, the journalistic ideals of telling the truth and serving the public good become harder to fulfill.

Another area where cost-conscious owners try to save money is on salaries. Salaries in journalism have historically been low, and despite the huge profits generated by newspapers and TV stations, show no signs of rising appreciably any time soon. One recent study found that starting pay for journalism graduates ranked last among 28 academic majors. Even worse, their salaries often remain below those of other professions. It is just assumed in the news business that what is missing in money is made up for by the thrills of the job.

But the assumption may well be wrong. Low salaries make it unlikely that the best young minds will choose journalism as a career or stay in it if they do. A survey released in 1992 by the Freedom Forum reported that over 20 percent of journalists said they were planning to leave the profession, with the "more experienced and altruistic" being the most disgruntled. Everette E. Dennis, executive director of the Freedom Forum Media Studies Center, warns that unless newsroom conditions improve, news organizations are likely to end up with journalists "who are not as smart, not as accomplished, more compliant, more malleable." These, of course, aren't exactly the type to inspire confidence in the future of a free and public-spirited press.

Media ethicists Philip Patterson and Lee Wilkins suggest that "one way to learn ethics is to select heroes and to try to model your individual acts and ultimately your professional character on what you believe they would do." In a similar vein, philosopher Sissela Bok has proposed that people consult one of their heroes as an expert when making an ethical choice. Ironically, in *Eight Men Out*, the leaders to whom people might reasonably be expected to look for moral guidance are themselves morally bankrupt.

We have already seen how Comiskey takes selfish advantage of his position and power. Ban Johnson, president of the American League, is portrayed as really no better at fulfilling a leadership role. After the White Sox drop the first two games of the series, their field manager, William "Kid" Gleason (John Mahoney), goes to Comiskey with rumors of a fix. A wildly agitated Comiskey wakes up Johnson in the middle of the night, demanding that he do something. But Johnson, who is feuding with Comiskey over another matter, refuses to stop the series or even investigate the rumors. He prefers instead to watch Comiskey writhe in frustration. If there is a lesson here, it is that sins of omission (not acting when you should) can be just as bad as sins of commission (acting in ways you shouldn't).

Of all the designated leaders in the film, Gleason is the easiest to identify with. His position as manager is roughly equivalent to that of a supervisory editor in the newsroom—the copy desk chief, for example, or the city editor. As editors usually come from the ranks of reporters, Gleason comes from the ranks of players, having been a star pitcher in his day. And as editors are sometimes required by their job to implement policies they personally dislike, he must carry out Comiskey's unfair initiatives and edicts. His lack of autonomy is illustrated in the scene in which the White Sox players receive stale champagne as their bonus for winning the pennant. "Fellas," Gleason says apologetically, "if it was up to me." But it isn't, and the question becomes whether that is his fault.

Should Gleason have better defended his players against Comiskey? Did he allow fear for his job to weaken his commitment to justice? His pep talk to the team before the first game of the series reveals his nervous awareness that players may try to redress their grievances by dishonest means: "I'm hearing a lot about odds lately, like this is a race track, everyone's a damn handicapper. Well, sometimes the smart money gets a little too smart for its own good. But I'll tell ya, I've been in this game over thirty years, and I've never yet seen a club that could hold a candle to you fellas. That's the straight dope. The way I figure, we can't be beaten. We can only beat ourselves. You fellas know what I mean. All right, lets get 'em."

The players respond to this traditional appeal to pride and team-work by going out and throwing the game. Unwilling to risk his job to protect them from a cruel and arbitrary owner, Gleason has lost his credibility as a leader, his power to guide and inspire. He still has his management position, but is it a position still worth having? Whether on the ball field or in the newsroom, managers might do well to remember what many ethicists have said—it is better to be on the side of the persecuted than of the persecutors.

THE BRAZEN RULE

According to *Eight Men Out*, White Sox players joined the fix to get even with team owner Charles Comiskey for squeezing their salaries and skunking them out of bonuses. Perhaps none had more reason to want to get even than veteran pitcher Eddie Cicotte, whom Comiskey had promised a $10,000 bonus if he won thirty games that season. In the film, when Cicotte (David Strathairn) comes by Comiskey's office to collect the bonus, Comiskey refuses to pay it, noting that Cicotte won only twenty-nine games. "You had Kid bench me for two whole weeks in August," Cicotte protests. "I missed five starts." But Comiskey is adamant. "Twenty-nine is not thirty, Eddie," he says. "You will get only the money you deserve." Immediately after the meeting, Cicotte agrees to join the fix. His price is $10,000—the exact amount of his promised bonus—up front.

Are Cicotte and his teammates justified in repaying Comiskey's treachery with treachery of their own? The answer seems to largely depend on which ethical rule one applies to the situation. The Golden Rule, which the Reverend Davidson Loehr calls "the most famous ethical rule in the world," states, "Do unto others as you would have them do unto you," or, in plainer language, "Repay evil with kind-ness, and injustice with forgiveness." Measured by this rule, the White Sox players are dead wrong to return hurt for hurt, lie for lie.

But, as Loehr points out, history "shows that the Golden Rule has never been consistently followed by anybody anyway—certainly not by the powerful." Down through the ages, the rich and powerful have followed the Iron Rule: "Do unto others as you like, *before* they do it unto you." Comiskey himself follows this rule—also expressed as "He who has the gold makes the rules," or "Might makes right"—in dealing crookedly with his players.

By giving the same back to Comiskey, the players follow the Brazen Rule: "Do unto others as they do unto you." This rule is often attributed to Confucius, who when asked in the sixth century B.C. his opinion of the idealistic notion of repaying evil with kindness, responded, "Then with what will you repay kindness?" Loehr summarizes the Brazen Rule as "Repay kindness with kindness, but evil with justice."

Robert Axelrod, a political scientist at the University of Michigan, has examined these and other ethical rules through a series of interactive computer experiments, hoping to find which rules create the most stable and cooperative societies. Both the Golden Rule and the Iron Rule always fail the test—because of excessive kindness and excessive ruthlessness, respectively. The most constructive long-term strategy is a variation on the Brazen Rule called "Tit-for-Tat" in which you start with a kind act and then, in each subsequent round, just do what your opponent did the last time.

In *Eight Men Out*, however, following the Brazen Rule of treating others as they have treated you doesn't create more stability and cooperation. Quite the contrary. It creates social anarchy. Once some White Sox players decide to betray their teammates and manager and throw the series, no obligation is secure anymore, and betrayal becomes the order of the day. Gamblers betray players, players betray gamblers, gamblers betray each other—and all betray the public, who trust in the honesty and integrity of the old ball game.

How is it that the Brazen Rule miscarries so badly? Why does following the rule lead to less, not more, ethical behavior in the film? The reason may be that behavioral rules—and, in the case of journalists, newsroom codes of ethics—are simply abstractions that are only as good as the character of the people who interpret and apply them. The Brazen Rule works, when it works at all, by intimidation—the prospect that you will inevitably suffer the same damage you have inflicted. It rests not on empathy for potential victims or on a moral commitment to the rights of others, but on fear of reprisal. If you believe you can somehow escape reprisal for behaving unethically, then the Brazen Rule won't serve to stop you.

Ethical behavior grows out of empathy, which Bok defines as "the ability to feel with and for others and to respond to their suffering." Without empathy, Bok states, "there can be no beginnings of felt responsibility." The ethical person is one who recognizes that his or her acts reverberate in the larger world and tries, at the very least, to do no harm—a concept that has been part of medical ethics since Hippocrates in the fourth century B.C. Ethics isn't mainly about promulgating rules and regulations. It is about taking care of each other.

The Black Sox took care of themselves, and the result was a scandal from which baseball, America's game, only slowly recovered. We might ask whether journalists who put their rights before their responsibilities, or their careers before all else, pose a similar threat to the health of their profession. We might also ask whether, in this era of market-driven coverage and media self-merchandising, journalism has the will to widen its circle of empathy to encompass the underemployed as well as the upwardly mobile, the political left as well as the political right, the old and broken as well as the young and beautiful.

SMELLS LIKE TEAM SPIRIT

The World Series fix might never have occurred had certain star players—Cicotte, Williams, Jackson—not signed on. In *Eight Men Out*, infielders Gandil and Risberg, the organizers of the fix, get a couple of them to participate by appealing to their team spirit. For example, as a night train carries the White Sox to Cincinnati for the opening game of the series, Risberg (Don Harvey) explains the will of the team to Jackson (D. B. Sweeney), who can hit and field brilliantly, but can't read or write.

> *Risberg*: Listen, Joe, we got together, most of the guys, and the thing is, we're gonna drop a couple of games in the series.
>
> *Jackson*: Who?
>
> *Risberg*: Everybody. Chick, me, Cicotte, Lefty.
>
> *Jackson*: Lefty?
>
> *Risberg*: Sure, Lefty. And Fred and Hap and Bucky. Everybody. And Joe, some of 'em—well, I won't name names—but I had to tell 'em, 'No, we can't leave Joe out of this. He's one of us.' I says—
>
> *Jackson*: You want me?
>
> *Risberg*: We need you, Joe.
>
> *Jackson*: I don't know.
>
> *Risberg*: You'd be an awful sap to turn it down at this point, Joe. . . . I mean, it'd just be stupid not to do it. You don't want to be stupid, do you, Joe?
>
> *Jackson*: I don't know.

Risberg: People are gonna be awful pissed if you fuck up their plans, Joe. You don't want to piss everybody off, do you, Joe, huh? You don't want *me* mad at you, do you?

Jackson: Everybody else is in?

Risberg: Everybody we need.

Jackson: Okay.

Risberg: There's a good boy.

Joe finds it impossible, despite clearly having misgivings about the fix, to resist the pull of team loyalty. From an early age, most of us are taught to subordinate our own egos to the group or groups to which we belong. We are told, "There is no 'I' in team." We have ground into our heads the notion that success requires a "team effort." We come to accept the term "team player" as a compliment.

But is teamwork a virtue under all circumstances? Exactly how much loyalty is owed teammates who, like the Black Sox, plan to betray the public trust? John C. Merrill, professor emeritus of journalism at the University of Missouri, Columbia, points out that "many cohesive social groups are evil, and if individualism means standing apart from such groups, then individualism can be quite a good thing."

In the film, third baseman Buck Weaver (John Cusack) struggles with the question of where his loyalties should lie. Although considered "one of the boys" and brought in on the fix, Weaver is a fierce competitor who hates to lose. He makes a diving backhand stop on a hard-hit ball early in the first game of the series, then jumps up and throws the batter out, leaving Gandil staring at him in puzzlement across the infield. After the game, which the Sox dump by a score of 9–1, Risberg wanders over to Weaver's locker for a heart-to-heart.

Risberg: So what's the story, Buck?

Weaver: What does it look like?

Risberg: Looks like you skunked out on us.

Weaver: I haven't taken a nickel. I don't owe anybody a damn thing.

Risberg: We let you in on the meetings.

Weaver: Look, you just play your ball game, and I'll play mine, and we'll see how it comes out.

Just as Weaver draws a line at dumping games, he draws another line at squealing on his teammates. He continues to be loyal to them in his own mind by not disclosing the fix to his manager or reporters or the league president. His silence, however, brings him into conflict with yet other loyalties he has accumulated as a professional ballplayer, including to the team owner who pays his wages and to the fans who pay admission to the stadium.

Clifford G. Christians, Kim B. Rotzoll, and Mark Fackler observe in their book *Media Ethics: Cases and Moral Reasoning* that we all carry around an assortment of personal and professional loyalties, and that often "the most agonizing dilemmas" concern choosing to whom our primary loyalty is owed. "Policies and actions," they write, "inevitably must favor some [person or group] to the exclusion of others." But Weaver never seems to realize this. He acts as if he can maintain his honor and integrity while protecting his cheating teammates—a contradiction in terms.

Where should Weaver's loyalties lie? Probably with the public that follows baseball. It is their money and interest that support the game and make his career possible. He gives them a sincere effort on the field, but he owes them something more. He owes them the truth, which is that the fix is on. And he owes the same to players throughout the majors. Rather than wishing that the corruption would just go away, Weaver has a duty to his colleagues on other teams to help preserve high professional standards. All the records of all the players who ever played major league ball become suspect if the game is, or is even perceived to be, under the control of gamblers.

The loyalty issues raised by the film aren't unlike those confronting the press. Christians, Rotzoll, and Fackler identify five types of obligation that journalists must negotiate: duty to ourselves; duty to clients/subscribers/supporters; duty to our organization or firm; duty to professional colleagues; and duty to society. They put special emphasis on the duty to ourselves, noting that "following our conscience may be the best alternative in many situations." Other ethicists agree. Merrill, for example, states, "Reporters who, due to their individual consciences, refuse to go along with the group-mandated activities of their newspapers, are not necessarily wrong in their ethics and may very well be right."

Nonetheless, ethicists generally give first priority to a journalist's duty to society. As James Carey, a professor at Columbia University's Graduate School of Journalism, writes, "Insofar as journalism is grounded, it is grounded in the public; insofar as journalism has a client, the client is the public. . . . Ethics in journalism originates and flows from the relationship of the press to the public." In the same way the ballplayers in *Eight Men Out* owe their fans an honest effort, journalists owe their audience an honest story, one that truly gets to the bottom of things, rather than just scratches the surface or tells the official version. Ethical journalists are committed to trying to replace ignorance with understanding, brutality with empathy. They define themselves not as loyal employees or as privileged professionals, but as public representatives. Their hearts are open, and they don't work only for a paycheck. They work because the night is coming.

IN THE NEWS

Among the secondary characters in *Eight Men Out* are sportswriters Ring Lardner and Hughie Fullerton, the former played with dour intensity by Sayles and the latter with sardonic humor by bestselling author Studs Terkel. One reviewer observed, aptly, that the pair "wander through the film as a tiny Greek chorus," recording and lamenting the Black Sox scandal. In real life, Lardner was so disillusioned by the fix that he stopped covering baseball, even stopped going to ball games. The disillusionment contributed to his bitter portrayal of ballplayers in later short stories like "Alibi Ike" and "You Know Me, Al."

As for the real-life Fullerton, a columnist for the *Chicago Herald and Examiner*, he reported—some claim "invented"—one of the best-known lines to come out of American sports: "Say it ain't so, Joe." *Eight Men Out* presents the moment much as Fullerton described it in a widely syndicated column in September 1920. Jackson, "guarded like a felon by other men," emerges from the courthouse after giving grand jury testimony. A crowd has gathered on the steps and sidewalk, and from its midst a little blond boy, the epitome of the adoring fan, calls out the famous plea. Joe looks silently down at the boy, then turns away in shame. Fullerton wrote that it wasn't until Joe saw the anguish on the boy's face that he understood "the enormity of the thing he had done."

In the film, Lardner and Fullerton begin early on to suspect that players may be colluding with gamblers. At the ballpark before the start of the first game of the series, they question Gleason about disturbing rumors they have heard.

Gleason: I heard the same thing, fellas. Every series I've been to there are rumors of a fix just to shake up the odds. Hang out in bars you hear a lot of screwy things.

Lardner: Doesn't mean they're not true.

Gleason: My guys would've told me somethin' was up.

Fullerton: Sure they would, Kid. Give them hell out there.

But as soon as Gleason is out of earshot, Fullerton tells Lardner, "Let's keep separate scorecards. You circle every play that smells fishy, I'll do the same. We'll compare them after the game."

The ethical orientation of these journalists is apparent from even this brief scene. Lardner and Fullerton have what Ernest Hemingway, who himself began his literary career as a journalist, said all writers should have—"a built-in, shockproof bullshit detector." They refuse to be lulled into complacency by official assurances. Rather, they think independently and act without fear or favor.

At the same time, however, they avoid the occupational hazard of being overly adversarial, of always suspecting the worst of everyone. After Cicotte pitches uncharacteristically bad in the series opener, Lardner invites him to his hotel room and says point-blank, "I want to know if the series is on the level, Eddie." Cicotte answers that it is. A few days later, he dumps another game, and Lardner watching from the press box mutters, "You lied to me, Eddie." He sounds genuinely surprised and hurt. Despite his cool, almost catatonic demeanor and the notorious cynicism of his profession, he retains the capacity to trust in and empathize with others, and to feel let down by them.

Eight Men Out portrays Lardner and Fullerton as exceptional journalists, the sort who go beyond the superficiality of routine press coverage, who embody what Patterson and Wilkins call "ethical news values," such as accuracy ("using the correct facts and the right words and putting things in context"), tenacity ("knowing when a story is important enough to require additional effort"), equity ("treating all sources and subjects equally"), and community ("evaluating stories with an eye to social good first"). In fact, the film suggests that if it weren't for Fullerton's commitment to the truth, the fix probably would never have been uncovered. Sitting in the deserted press box with Lardner after the White Sox drop the series, he takes out a team picture and draws circles around the players he suspects of being crooked.

Fullerton: These five, maybe more.

Lardner: You prove it this town will never forgive you.

Fullerton: Yep.

The film then segues into a montage of Fullerton interviewing catcher Ray Schalk (Gordon Clapp) at a gym and small-time hood Billy Maharg (Richard Edson) in a bar, as well as of the reporter, hat on head, using the venerable two-finger method to type the resulting story. Also included in the sequence are shots of Cicotte and Weaver reading the newspaper (Jackson has it read to him by his wife), their expressions alternating between disbelief at public exposure of the fix and worry about their own fate.

But, as Lardner predicted, Fullerton's findings are angrily challenged, and not least by the rest of the Chicago press, which suffers from a severe case of local boosterism. Front-page headlines scream, "Cheap Shots Plague Players" and "Sour Grapes," while editorials denounce Fullerton and his kind as "leeches, sucking the lifeblood of honest sportsmen." These papers aren't interested in telling the truth; they are interested in increasing their circulation. They are cheerleaders for the most popular side of any controversy.

The press is always being criticized for its sensationalism, but its lack of courage is as large a problem. News organizations have a strong financial incentive to not antagonize their audiences, to not get too far ahead of their readers' or viewers' values. Wayne Ezell, editor of the *Boca Raton News*, spoke for many newsroom managers when he admitted recently, "If readers said they wanted more comics and less foreign news, in a market-driven economy, I'm going to give them more comics and less foreign news."

Important stories can easily get trampled in the rush to give the public what it wants. Veteran journalist Richard Reeves, looking back on his long, distinguished career, notes that the press showed up late—sometimes quite a bit late—on the big stories of the past forty years: the struggle for civil rights, the antiwar movement, feminism, environmentalism, religious revival. It was the obscure Pacific News Service, not the omnipresent Associated Press, that had the guts to expose the My Lai massacre by U.S. soldiers in Vietnam, and it was two cub reporters, not the White House press corps, who took the initiative to pursue the Watergate scandal. Is the mainstream press any better now about telling unpopular stories? And which stories are these today? And who misses them if they go untold? Who even knows they are missing?

AND JUSTICE FOR ALL

Audiences are supposed to get the feeling while watching *Eight Men Out* that the ballplayers were scapegoated. So far as the film is concerned, the real villains in the Black Sox scandal were the baseball establishment and the group of gamblers led by Arnold Rothstein (Michael Lerner) and including Abe Attell (Michael Mantell) and Sullivan. Yet it is the players who end up punished, banned from professional baseball for life. In one of the most moving speeches in the film, Cicotte rails against the unfairness of the situation: "I always figured it was talent that made a man big—you know, if you were the best at somethin.' We're the guys they come to see. Without us, there ain't a ball game. Yeah, but look who's holding the money and look who's facing the jail cell. Talent don't mean nothin,' and where's Comiskey and Sullivan, Attell, Rothstein? Out in the back room, cutting up the profits, that's where. That's the damn conspiracy."

The film portrays the judicial process as a charade, stage-managed by sleek lawyers on fat retainers and operated for the secret benefit of the rich and powerful. Once the scandal breaks in the press, Comiskey hires the best lawyer around, Albert Austrian, who points out, "Some kind of investigation is going to be launched. Our job is to control that investigation—in fact, to appear to be leading it." He takes advantage of the players' trust, cajoling Cicotte and Jackson, for example, into cooperating with the grand jury and into signing full confessions.

Just before the players go on trial, Austrian meets with an emissary from Rothstein, a scene without a proven historical basis, but inserted by writer-director Sayles to emphasize the parallels between the business world and the underworld. "Mr. Rothstein feels he and your Mr. Comiskey have certain interests in common," the emissary explains. "Negative publicity can be very bad for both of their businesses." Austrian cuts through the verbiage and asks what Rothstein wants. "Confessions" is the terse reply. Later, when the players' confessions are reported missing during the trial, this meeting suddenly takes on a dark, retrospective importance.

A jury ends up acquitting the Black Sox—"That was a bigger fix than the series," Lardner says—but the players aren't home free.

Landis (John Anderson), a former federal judge and the new com-missioner of baseball, immediately bans them from the game. Over shots of the players carousing with the jurors at a posttrial party, Landis reads his edict on the soundtrack as if the voice of doom: "Regardless of the verdict of juries, no player who throws a ball game, no player who undertakes or promises to throw a ball game, no player who sits in conference with a bunch of crooked players where the ways and means of throwing a ball game are discussed and does not promptly tells his club about it, will ever play professional baseball."

Is it fair that the players are banned for life from the game they loved? Did Landis, who had been granted absolute power over base-ball by team owners, act arbitrarily? Where is the justice in the players being punished while the owners escape all responsibility for the rotten state of things? At the press conference announcing Landis's appointment, Fullerton whispers to Lardner, "He says he's going to clean up baseball," and Lardner, nodding toward the owners, cracks, "He can start with those birds up on the stairs with him."

He doesn't, of course, and because he doesn't, we are left to won-der if banning the players is just. We know by now the extenuating circumstances surrounding the fix and have seen the gamblers sneak away with most of the money. We feel the players—those poor dupes—deserve sympathy. Yet when all is said and done, they may also deserve banishment.

Professional baseball depends for its survival on fan support, and fan support depends, in turn, on the presumed integrity of the game. There is no room in baseball for shirkers and cheaters or for those who willingly abide them. Fans expect the competition on the field to be authentic. It is why they click through the turnstiles, why they root for the home team, why they argue over players' statistics. The Black Sox scandal tarnished the reputation of baseball. Landis was hired to restore public confidence, and he did it in one bold stroke—by banning the suspect players. He might have done more, but do-ing any less would have been unjust to the millions of fans who support the game with their money and attention.

Journalism presents an analogous situation. The general rule, to quote the trade magazine *Editor and Publisher*, is that "any suspi-cions about honesty automatically make a reporter unsuitable for the job." In 1999 the *Owensboro (Kentucky) Messenger-Inquirer*, a thirty-one-thousand-circulation newspaper, fired reporter Kim Stacey for lying in a string of stories about her health problems. Earlier the same year, the *Boston Globe* asked columnist Mike Barnicle to resign amid charges of plagiarism and fabrication. Another *Globe* columnist, Patricia Smith, left the paper after admitting that she made up characters and quotes. "It is considered the major sin by journalists, and it should be," says Deni Elliott, a former *Philadelphia Inquirer* reporter and director of the Practical Ethics Center at the University of Montana. Orville Schell, dean of the Graduate School of Journalism at the University of California, Berkeley, agrees. "It is reprehensible when people falsify the public media," he says. "It risks the trust" of the audience.

There is no higher goal for journalists than telling the truth—and no harder one for them to reach. They must find the truth by the next deadline and report it in the limited space available. They must pry it from duplicitous sources and secretive governments, and communicate it to the public despite contrary commercial pressures. And they must guard all the while against allowing their own opinions and assumptions to color the story. It is an impossible job in many ways. What is possible, however, is to undertake it with honesty. If journalists can't always find or tell the whole truth, they can at least always be honest in their attempt to do so. Truth is abstract and elusive; honesty is personal and achievable.

THE PURSUIT OF UNHAPPINESS

Why be ethical? Why not lie and cheat and take advantage of others? "You don't play the angles," Gandil says early in *Eight Men Out*, "you're a sap." Maybe, but some of the Black Sox eventually come to regret joining the fix, and not just because the gamblers won't pay up. On the eve of his third start in the series, Cicotte is resting on the bed in his hotel room when fellow pitcher Lefty Williams (James Read) knocks and enters.

Williams: How's it going?

Cicotte: Okay.

Williams: Still no word from Chick about the money.

Cicotte: I don't care about the money.

Williams: Yeah. Peculiar way to find that out, isn't it?

Cicotte and Williams now realize that they have betrayed more than their team owner and their fans. They have betrayed their talent—a kind of suicide.

Classical philosophers as different as Immanuel Kant and John Stuart Mill believe that people have a duty to develop their talent. In *On Liberty*, Mill writes, "Men should act to the best of their ability. There is no . . . absolute certainty, but there is assurance sufficient for the purposes of human life." Contemporary ethicist Vincent Di Norcia, drawing on Mill's philosophy, proposes "Act, learn, improve" as an important maxim to follow. "One must monitor, learn from mistakes, practice, tinker, experiment, and refine one's performance," he says. "And one must do one's best."

We occasionally glimpse in *Eight Men Out* the satisfaction that comes from doing one's best. When the film opens, for example, the White Sox are still giving free reign to their abilities. Batters stroke timely hits; infielders turn graceful double plays; and outfielders make spectacular running catches. After one such catch to end an inning, Felsch (Charlie Sheen) jogs in from center field. "Jesus, Hap," Gleason greets him, "save it, will ya." "Save it for what?" Felsch asks. Baseball is these players' lives as well as their livelihood, and they play it with joyful abandon.

The joy begins to fade the very moment they join the fix. Their play, once so phenomenal, becomes painful for even their families to watch. Cicotte's wife and two young daughters sit in the stands beaming when he takes the mound for the first game of the series. But he then proceeds to disgrace his talent, intentionally giving up run after run. His wife turns her face away and hugs the girls to her body, as if shielding them from the sight of something obscene.

Eight Men Out elegizes "a bunch of dumb ballplayers" (Cicotte's phrase) who mistake revenge for justice, and money and the things it can buy for happiness. As Joel J. Kupperman states in his book *Character*, "To equate happiness with pleasure is not only to simplify the goals of life, but also to leave out . . . the individual's sense of self. . . . If one's sense of self is unsatisfactory, happiness is out of the question." Having agreed to throw the World Series, the players lose more than a few games—they lose their self-respect. "The dugout," Weaver admits to his wife, "it's like no one can look each other in the eye." For all their apparent toughness, the players are too conscience-stricken to be crooked and happy at the same time.

In his book, Kupperman endorses Aristotle's view that a person's degree of happiness "depended heavily on that person's possession and exercise of excellences, including intellectual abilities and . . . moral virtues." What does this mean for journalists? First, that they should find happiness in their work, not in the money and prestige attached to it; second, that they should always strive to reach their full potential; and third, that they should avoid entangling alliances—for example, with sources or advertisers—that would compromise their freedom of expression.

Rarely do people face the kind of big decision the eight White Sox faced when asked to throw the series. Nor usually does one bad ethical choice have the kind of catastrophic consequences theirs did, destroying their careers and forever ruining their reputations. Most of us go through our professional lives so caught up in the routine details of our jobs that ethical issues don't even register as such. But in a world crowded with fast new machines and increasingly dominated by corporate money, we should perhaps pay greater attention to our priorities. It is easy to hurt others or to get hurt ourselves, easy to misplace what writer Max Eastman years ago called "the true values of life." Why be ethical? The broken dreams of the banished players tell us why.

QUESTIONS TO CONSIDER

1. Are there parallels between baseball players' obligations to fans and journalists' obligations to readers? Describe these obligations in ethical terms. Did the players in *Eight Men Out* live up to their obligations? Did the journalists?

2. "You don't play the angles," first baseman Chick Gandil says in the film, "you're a sap." Would it be acceptable for media workers to adopt this maxim? Explain your response.

3. To whom do the players in *Eight Men Out* owe loyalty? To the team? Their employer? The gamblers? Their fans? Can they maintain a variety of loyalties at the same time? Do some loyalties take precedence over others? Which ones and why?

4. Is teamwork a positive or negative force in the film? Does belonging to a team or professional group necessarily mean going along with all the decisions and activities of the group?

5. Can baseball—or media professions—abide cheaters? Or, to put it another way, was banning the Black Sox the right thing to do?

6. Which characters in the film qualify as role models? To whom could one look for ethical advice or moral example?

FURTHER READING

Asinof, Eliot. *Eight Men Out*. New York: Henry Holt, 1963.

Bok, Sissela. *Mayhem: Violence As Public Entertainment*. Reading, Mass.: Addison-Wesley, 1998.

Carey, James. "Journalists Just Leave: The Ethics of an Anomalous Profession." In *The Media and Morality*, ed. Robert M. Baird, William E. Loges, and Stuart E. Rosenbaum. New York: Prometheus, 1999.

Chicago Historical Society, <http://www.chicagohs.org/history/blacksox.html

Christians, Clifford G., Kim B. Rotzoll, and Mark Fackler. *Media Ethics: Cases and Moral Reasoning*. 4th ed. New York: Longman, 1995.

Davis, Thulani. "Blue-Collar Auteur." *American Film* (June 1991): 19–23, 49–50.

Di Norcia, Vincent. *Hard Like Water: Ethics in Business*. Toronto: Oxford University Press Canada, 1998.

Goodwin, Gene, and Ron F. Smith. *Groping for Ethics in Journalism*. 3rd ed. Ames: Iowa State University Press, 1994.

Gropman, Donald. *Say It Ain't So, Joe!: The Story of Shoeless Joe Jackson*. Boston: Little, Brown, 1979.

Kupperman, Joel J. *Character*. New York: Oxford University Press, 1991.

Merrill, John C. *Journalism Ethics: Philosophical Foundations for News Media*. New York: St. Martin's, 1997.

Patterson, Philip, and Lee Wilkins, ed. *Media Ethics: Issues and Cases*. 3rd ed. Boston: McGraw-Hill, 1998.

Reeves, Richard. *What the People Know: Freedom and the Press*. Cambridge, Mass.: Harvard University Press, 1998.

Sherrill, Robert. "News Ethics: Press and Jerks." *Grand Street* (Winter 1986): 115–133.

8

True Crime: The Good, the Bad, and the Journalist

Steve Everett, the reporter-hero of *True Crime*, seems throughout most of the 1999 film to be anything but heroic. Played by Clint Eastwood, who also directed the picture, Everett was fired from a New York paper for screwing around with the publisher's underage daughter ("She looked eighteen to me," he lamely offers in excuse). Now working in comparative obscurity at the *Oakland Tribune*, he continues to make a mess of both his personal life and his career. He is a former drunk who hangs out in bars; a married man who sleeps with his city editor's wife; and a muckraker who gets splattered by the muck he rakes up. Before he quit the bottle two months ago, he led a crusade to clear accused rapist Mike Vargas that ended embarrassingly—with Vargas confessing when threatened with a DNA test. "I'm surprised they didn't fire you on the spot," another character says. "So am I," Everett admits.

True Crime gives Everett an opportunity to redeem himself. When a young female colleague dies in a drunk-driving accident—just after he tries to seduce her—he inherits what would have been her story about the last hours of Frank Beachum (Isaiah Washington), a black man on death row for killing a white convenience store clerk. Everett, whose once-unerring nose for news has been blunted by his drinking, smells something rotten here. He begins a race against time to save Beachum.

This plot, as critic Stanley Kauffmann noted somewhat crankily in the *New Republic*, is "antique." The granddaddy of all newspaper films, *The Front Page* (1931), follows the frantic and often humorous efforts of reporter Hildy Johnson (Pat O'Brien) and editor Walter Burns (Adolphe Menjou) to rescue a muddleheaded anarchist from the noose on the very eve of his hanging. *Call Northside 777* (1948), another classic of the genre, presents a reporter named McNeil (James Stewart) who fights to free a man serving a life sentence for a murder he didn't commit. But *True Crime* is different from these earlier films in at least one crucial respect. While the other films have heroes that brim with self-confidence, *True Crime*'s hero is riddled with guilt.

Everett can recognize when he has had a lapse of judgment or ethics. He says at various points in the film that he is sorry for allowing his young female colleague to drive off drunk; for dumping his daughter out of a stroller during a hurried visit to the zoo; for cuckolding the city editor; for endangering his own marriage; and for nearly drowning his career in booze. "Bad people," Aristotle observes, "are full of regrets," and by this measure, Everett is bad. But is he bad to the extent of being evil?

Aristotle distinguishes between the morally evil person and the morally weak person. The morally evil person, on the one hand, chooses to behave badly because his practical reasoning is corrupt; he can't recognize that what seems good isn't genuinely good. Thinking that it is right to pursue pleasure to excess, he feels no remorse for the way he acts. The morally weak person, on the other hand, suffers pangs of conscience over his behavior. As Roger J. Sullivan, an expert on Aristotelian ethics, explains, the morally weak person can feel remorse because he doesn't "deny rightness and the binding force of moral principles. Consequently, there is hope that his moral illness can be cured."

Ethics sometimes seems a forbidding subject, too difficult for anyone but philosophers or prospective saints. In addition, the struggle to identify the best ethical values and abide by them strikes not a few people as futile, given the darkness of human nature and the chaotic state of the world. But the interesting thing about *True Crime* is that it raises the possibility that even a morally weak person can grope his way to a good act. And if someone like Everett can do it, then why can't we?

THE CALL OF DUTY

It isn't always apparent what kind of moral reasoning Everett is using in *True Crime*. Many of us, including those who have never heard of Jeremy Bentham or John Stuart Mill, are utilitarians. We weigh the rightness or wrongness of an action by considering its consequences. In fact, Edmund B. Lambeth notes that utilitarianism—the philosophy of "the greatest good for the greatest number," generally attributed to Bentham and Mill—is "the news media's predominant mode of moral reasoning."

But there are problems with this approach, as Lambeth, among other ethicists, recognizes. "When does the rubbery yardstick of 'the greatest good for the greatest number,'" he asks, "become a figleaf, a shibboleth, to justify use of flagrant deception or massive invasion of privacy in order to 'get the story' for the majority?" The question implies that bringing about the greatest amount of good isn't necessarily the only morally relevant characteristic of an action.

Arthur C. Dyck has developed a scenario to illustrate this. A house is on fire. Inside it are a medical genius and your mother or father. You can save only one person from the flames. Which one will it be?

Utilitarians would save the medical genius. Restricting their reasoning to a consideration of possible benefits, they would conclude that saving the medical genius will result in the greatest good for the greatest number. He or she might find a cure for cancer or some other deadly disease. What is your mother or father likely to find? Your lamentable grade report in the mail?

Such reasoning rests on several shaky assumptions. First, it assumes that the medical genius, if saved, will inevitably fulfill his or her genius, which may not be the case; premature death or lack of funds or simple bad luck could intervene. Second, it assumes that his or her genius will be applied to beneficial ends, but the records of gruesome medical experiments conducted by Nazi doctors on death-camp inmates demonstrate just how insupportable that assumption is. Third and last, it assumes that the future is the only point of reference for an action, overlooking the fact that there are also, in Dyck's words, "relationships to the past that are morally significant"—for example, having made a promise or having wronged someone.

W. D. Ross, an influential modern critic of utilitarianism, argues that we have to recognize "the *intrinsic* rightness of a certain type of act," apart from any consequences. "When a plain man fulfills a promise because he thinks he ought to do so," Ross writes in

The Right and the Good, "it seems clear that he does so with no thought of its total consequences, still less with any opinion that these are likely to be the best possible. He thinks in fact much more of the past than of the future. What makes him think it right to act in a certain way is the fact that he had promised to do so—that and, usually, nothing more." Ross insists that promise-keeping is "a *prima facie* duty," something incumbent on a person and right by its very nature. "That which is right is right," he says, "not because it is an act, one thing, which will produce another thing, an increase of the general welfare, but because it is itself the producing of an increase in the general welfare."

Ross identifies six types of prima facie duties:

1. Some duties arise from previous acts of our own. These include *duties of fidelity*, which arise from previous promises, explicit or implicit. (An example of the latter is the promise not to tell lies implicit in writing articles that purport to be journalism and not fiction.) They also include *duties of reparation*, which arise from a previous wrongful act.

2. Some duties arise from services done to us by others. These are *duties of gratitude*.

3. Some duties arise from the fact or mere possibility of an unfair distribution of pleasure or happiness. These are *duties of justice*, according to which we should upset or prevent such a distribution.

4. Some duties arise from the fact that there are others in the world whose condition we can better in terms of virtue, intelligence, or pleasure. These are *duties of beneficence*.

5. Some duties arise from the fact that we can better our own condition in terms of virtue or intelligence. These are *duties of self-improvement*.

6. Ross states one duty in a negative way—*nonmaleficence*, the duty of "not injuring others."

If we return now to Dyck's burning house with this list in mind, we can see that we have a greater duty to rescue our parent than the medical genius. It is our parent, not the genius, who brought us into the world and sustained us through our vulnerable years. These previous acts of love and nurture create a moral claim on us, a duty of gratitude, and we are bound by what is self-evidently right to fulfill it.

The concept of duty probably seems odd, even oppressive, to many Americans today. We live in a consumer culture whose vision of the good life, sanctioned by popular therapies and reinforced through advertising, consists of unlimited purchasing power, immediate gratification of every impulse, and personal happiness and well being. "Self-absorption defines the moral climate of contemporary society," scholar Christopher Lasch notes. "The conquest of nature and the search for new frontiers has given way to the search for self-fulfillment." Utilitarianism fits neatly into this narcissistic cultural setting, for it says, in effect, that we stand in relation to each other not as promisee to promiser, or neighbor to neighbor, or child to parent, but only as possible beneficiaries of each others' actions.

There is nothing wrong per se with seeking self-gratification or pleasure. Most philosophers allow for it in their philosophies. The problem arises, as Ross contends, when the search for pleasure interferes with more important duties.

What are these more important duties for journalists? It depends on who you ask. The SPJ, the ASNE, the RTNDA, and the like recommend in their codes of ethics that journalists be honest, accurate, and fair. Meanwhile, some contemporary writers and teachers have attempted to adapt classical ethical theories—Aristotle's Golden Mean, Immanuel Kant's Categorical Imperative, and Mill's Principle of Utility—to journalism. Others have developed their own lists of journalistic duties and responsibilities. Lambeth, for example, suggests that journalists are "best guided" by the principles of "telling the truth, behaving justly, respecting and protecting independence and freedom, acting humanely, and being a good steward of the resources, especially the First Amendment, that protect journalism and a free society."

Ross never claims that his list of prima facie duties is complete or final. Instead of exhaustively cataloging duties, he goes on to examine how to decide which duty to follow. "When I am in a situation," he writes, "as perhaps I always am, in which more than one of these *prima facie* duties is incumbent on me, what I have to do is to study the situation as fully as I can until I form the considered opinion (it is never more) that in the circumstances one of them is more incumbent than any other." He emphasizes that the one duty is more incumbent not because it will "produce more good," but because it is in the circumstances "more of a duty."

A brief illustration should make clear what Ross means. Your professor has promised to meet you in her office at a certain hour, but breaks the appointment because she stops to help the victim of an accident. Ross would say she did the right thing. The duty to relieve distress is more binding in the circumstances than the duty to keep a trivial promise.

The moral complexity of *True Crime* can best be appreciated by placing the film within the framework of Ross's theory of multiple duties. As we will see, Everett attends to Beachum, the condemned man, and not to his own wife and daughter or to his editor, all of whom he owes duties of reparation because of previous wrongful acts. And so even though he does good by averting a miscarriage of justice, there is still a feeling of uneasiness, as if something important has been forgotten. He may fulfill one prima facie duty, but it is at the cost of not fulfilling another, or two others.

DEFYING MANAGEMENT

Bob Woodward, half of the reporting team that broke the Watergate scandal, once said, "All good work is done in defiance of management." Everett's experiences in *True Crime* seem to largely bear this out. He investigates the Beachum case despite the warnings—and to the eye-rolling exasperation—of city editor Bob Findley (Denis Leary).

Even though Findley assigns Everett to cover Beachum's execution, he does so only at the insistence of editor-in-chief Alan Mann (James Woods). "Everything with Everett is a big investigative witch-hunt, like the Mike Vargas piece," Findley complains. And as if that botch weren't enough to disillusion him, Everett is having an affair with his wife. When Findley confronts Everett about the affair, cornering the reporter in the supply room, Everett abjectly apologizes. "If it helps any," he says in a thick voice, "I feel awful." "Doesn't help," Findley replies.

What would help? How can Everett make amends to Findley—or, in Ross's terms, fulfill his duties of reparation? He might begin by following the city editor's instructions to the letter. "Don't pull a Dick Tracy on this, okay?" Findley warns. "I don't want some big investigative piece." "You can depend on that, don't worry," Everett says, then takes a closer look at the shoddy circumstantial evidence against Beachum. He is soon in Mann's office, begging to be allowed to go beyond routine execution-day coverage.

Where Findley is earnest and conservative, Mann is a throwback to the hot-tempered, circulation-crazy, shoot-from-the-lip editors who enlivened some of the greatest newspaper films ever made, such as *The Front Page*, *Nothing Sacred* (1936), and *His Girl Friday* (1940). In an early scene with Findley, Mann expounds with enormous zest his cynical philosophy of news: "Issues are shit we make up to give ourselves an excuse to run good stories. . . . Judge grabs a female attorney's tits. Hey, that's the sex discrimination *issue*. Nine-year-old boy blows away his brother with an Uzi—the child violence *issue*. People want to read about sex organs [Mann reaches for his crotch] and blood. We make up issues so they don't have to feel too nasty about it."

Now he treats Everett's hunch about Beachum with the same vulgar disdain. "Do you know my opinion of reporters who have hunches?" he asks. "I can't fart loud enough to express my opinion." Yet when Everett presses the point—"Alan, they're going to kill him tonight"—the big, bad editor shows a kind of gruff compassion. "I can't even tell you what'll happen if this turns into another Mike Vargas piece, okay?" Mann blusters. "So if you come up with something, fine, I'll run it, but . . . it had better be good."

On the one hand, then, Everett owes reparations to Findley. On the other hand, he owes gratitude to Mann for protecting him from Findley's animus and giving him a second chance. He can't fulfill his duty to Findley (do a routine execution story) without neglecting his duty to Mann (get the story behind the story). Further clouding the situation is the fact that, as Ross observes, duties are "compounded together in highly complex ways." For example, Everett's effort to clear Beachum rests not only on his implicit promise to Mann, but also on his obligation to tell the truth, improve himself, eliminate injustice, and better the condition of others; that is, the duty of gratitude is reinforced by the duties of fidelity, self-improvement, justice, and beneficence.

If this were everything involved, deciding which duties to carry out might not be so difficult, but Everett owes reparations to his long-suffering wife, Barbara (Diane Venora), as well as to Findley. His history of womanizing and boozing has left their marriage in shambles. After being assigned to the Beachum story, he phones her to say he will be home late. She reminds him that he promised to take their daughter to the zoo—another instance of "duties compounded together in highly complex ways."

Everett: Oh, the zoo. God, I forgot.

Barbara: Steve, she really is expecting you.

Everett: I'm sorry about that. I just forgot.

Barbara: Look, you worked all weekend. She didn't see you at all. You know how she loves her daddy. Steve, I know it's work, but I really think it'd be a bad idea to let her down like this again.

Guiltily aware of his previous wrongful acts, Everett manages to squeeze in a visit to the zoo between interviews. The result is a grotesque parody of parenting. In a hurry to get back to his story, he throws his daughter in a stroller and races by the animals at a dead run, but hits a sudden bump in the pavement, spilling her out. "Oh darling, I'm sorry," he says while other parents look on in horror. "I wouldn't have had this happen. Daddy's sorry." When he brings her home, Barbara gasps at the sight of her scrapes, then screams at him, "What the hell's the matter with you?" She pulls the girl inside and slams the door in his face.

The scene immediately shifts to San Quentin, where Beachum is saying his final good-byes to his wife, Bonnie (Lisa Gay Hamilton), and daughter under the eyes of armed guards. Imbued with love, natural dignity, and deep religious faith, the Beachums make an ironic contrast to the dysfunctional Everett clan. Also ironically, Everett helps the Beachum family at the cost of neglecting his own. Ross would argue that this is how things often work in actual experience.

True Crime is more than half over before Everett and Beachum meet for the first time, shaking hands through cell bars. "I guess you wanna hear how I feel to be in here," Beachum says and proceeds to describe his fears ("I feel . . . fear of pain, fear of prison, fear of being separated from my loved ones, all those fears rolled into one") and beliefs ("I believe in Jesus Christ, our Lord and savior. I believe that I'm going to a better place . . . , and there's better justice there"). When Beachum ends his recital, Everett, who has shown barely any interest in it, fixes him with a cool, appraising stare.

Everett: Mr. Beachum, you don't know me. I'm just a guy out there with a screw loose. Frankly, I don't give a rat's ass about Jesus Christ, and I don't care about justice in this world and the next. I don't even care what's right or wrong, never have. But you know what this is? [Everett touches his nose.]

Beachum: What is this, some kind of joke?

Everett: No, it's no joke. That's my nose. To tell ya the pitiful truth, that's all I have in life. And when my nose tells me something stinks, I got to have faith in it, just like you have faith in Jesus. When my nose is working well, I know there is truth out there somewhere, but if it isn't working well, then [Everett gives a rueful little laugh] they might as well drive me off a cliff because I'm nothing. Well, lately I'm not a hundred percent sure my nose has been really working that great. So I gotta ask ya, did you kill that woman or not?

As the audience learns from a dreamlike flashback, Beachum found the clerk lying behind the counter shot in the neck, and ran because he panicked, not because he robbed and killed her. Everett's nose is working well, but he will need harder evidence to stop the execution. "Give me something, goddamn it!" he shouts in frustration at Beachum. The guards use this as an excuse to throw the reporter out. Bonnie, who has been listening in the background with mounting hysteria, calls after him: "You believe us, don't you? Do you believe us? *Do you believe us?*"

Everett: Yes, I believe you

Bonnie [sobbing]: Then where were you? Dear God, where were you all this time?

Good question. And Everett answers it, while the guards drag him away, by saying, "It wasn't my story."

This raises the issue of news coverage. David J. Krajicek, a former reporter for the grubby *New York Post*, estimates that crime news accounts for one-third of the content of a typical daily paper and up to half of many local TV newscasts. But though plentiful, the coverage isn't the kind likely to enhance public understanding of the crime problem in a community. Most of it consists of what Krajicek describes as "raw dispatches about the crime of the moment." Such stories are cheap and easy to produce, which pleases media owners in an era ever more fixated on profits.

Everett's one-man crusade in *True Crime* challenges the tabloid mentality that now dominates news coverage, particularly on TV.

Throughout the film, we catch glimpses of TV reports about execution day, and they invariably display thoughtless clichés and stereotypes—an interview with the vengeful father of the murder victim, a sensational sound bite from a key prosecution witness, footage of death-penalty advocates demonstrating outside the prison. The implication is that what Everett must overcome to save Beachum isn't only the inertia of the criminal justice system, but also the prescriptive formulas of mass-market journalism.

Imagine for a moment that news stories came in different colors—red, green, yellow, blue, and so on. An editor who sends a reporter for, say, a red story expects the reporter to return with a red story. The editor has planned the next edition with the idea of red in mind. If the reporter brings back a green or blue story, the editor will be surprised and probably angry. The reporter might even be fired. The safest rule for reporters is, "Get what you are sent for," and most reporters play it safe.

Not Everett, though. To extend the previous metaphor, he prefers a color not found on his city editor's palette. Findley wants only a certain kind of story. "All I'm looking for," he says, "is the human interest, you know? Final days, what it's like, all right?" A little later, he repeats these instructions, as if Everett were a slow learner: "What I want you to do is interview Frank Beachum about his feelings today and turn it into a human-interest sidebar." But no matter how many times Findley tells him to hack out a human-interest story, Everett resists being confined by the narrow requirements of this popular journalistic genre. He is groping for a different kind of story when, following a hunch, he visits the store where the robbery-murder occurred six years ago. Pacing up and down and trying to visualize the crime, he asks a clerk about some marks on the floor.

Clerk: This in that story you're writing?

Everett: That's a good point. No, I'm writing a human-interest sidebar. Know what that is?

Clerk: No, I don't think I do.

Everett [snarling]: I don't think I do either.

Beachum may be wrongly executed in a few hours, and here is Everett under orders to not write a big investigative piece, but to just stick to formulaic coverage—the condemned man up close and personal. No wonder he sounds so ticked off. Under the circumstances, the human-interest sidebar is antihuman.

BETWEEN INTENTION AND ACTION

Everett ultimately overcomes family problems, the criminal justice system, an obstructive city editor, his own character flaws, and the journalistic form to save Beachum from execution. In an epilogue set during Christmas season, we learn from his lecherous banter with a pretty young cashier that he is back on top. He has a book deal and an inside track for the Pulitzer Prize, as well as a new divorce (but don't fret about his daughter—he has just bought her a stuffed animal). Stepping outside, he recognizes the Beachum family in the middle distance. The two men exchange meaningful glances. Then the camera pulls back to reveal the *Oakland Tribune* building towering protectively over the scene. It is a typical Hollywood ending in that it doesn't so much resolve the difficult issues—racism, capital punishment, crime coverage—raised by the film as obscure them in a happy glow.

But what if Everett had failed to save Beachum? At one point, the warden at San Quentin had cautioned him: "You know, these things go through all kinds of hearings and appeals before they get to us. It's no use trying to figure out who's naughty and who's nice, and then come sliding down the chimney like a hero, not on execution day. You're not Santa Claus. There's no such thing as Santa Claus." What if the warden had turned out to be right? What if Beachum had been executed—and there is a moment when the audience thinks he has—despite Everett's best efforts? Do good intentions count for anything? Would just the mere attempt to save Beachum have been considered a fulfillment of Everett's duties?

Different philosophers would answer differently. "Success and failure," Ross asserts, "are the only test, and a sufficient test, of the performance of duty." He cites the example of borrowing a book from a friend. "If I have promised to return the book to my friend," he says, "I obviously do not fulfill my promise and do not do my duty merely by aiming at his receiving the book; I must see that he actually receives it." In mailing the book back, Ross may have properly wrapped and addressed it and applied adequate postage, but his duty remains unfulfilled if the book never gets into his friend's hands. The fact that the book can get lost, mangled, or stolen in transit—all possibilities beyond his control—is no excuse: his friend still hasn't gotten the book. As Ross explains, "However likely my act may seem . . . to produce the result, if it does not produce it I have not done what I promised to do, i.e. have not done my duty." It isn't enough to have certain motives or intentions; we must do certain acts.

By contrast, Kant, considered the originator of duty-based ethics, argues that moral worth depends on a person's intentions, not on a person's accomplishments. He points out that we can't always accomplish what we wish because of our own limited abilities and uncooperative external conditions. The one thing we can always do, though, is to act in the right spirit. For Kant, this means acting from a sense of duty to some principle, with no regard for the consequences to ourselves or others. Remember the borrowed book? In Kant's universe, we would have done our duty if we made a sincere effort to return the book as promised. Whether the book actually got to where it was supposed to go would be irrelevant in determining the moral worth of the act.

Which of the two theories is the most useful? Which helps us better understand our experience in the world and our duties to each other? Both theories are quite stringent, with Kant requiring that we act with good will and Ross requiring that we see the act through to completion. There is no room in Kant's theory for commercial motives or in Ross's for half-hearted attempts or self-rationalizations. Under the latter theory, our duty isn't done until, like Everett, we get the story, expose the wrong, and end the injustice—until we finally keep the promise of a free and fearless press made long ago.

QUESTIONS TO CONSIDER

1. Does moral worth reside in a person's intentions, as Kant argues, or in a person's actions, as Ross claims? Which philosopher's version of duty-based ethics would provide a better foundation for journalism? Why?

2. Did Everett have a duty to follow or defy his city editor's instructions about covering execution day? Is it possible for newsrooms to operate efficiently if reporters can redefine their assignments at will? In what circumstances, if any, would a reporter be justified in ignoring an editor's orders?

3. Is editor-in-chief Alan Mann correct in saying, "People want to read about sex organs and blood. We make up issues so they

don't have to feel too nasty about it"? Whether you agree or disagree with him, illustrate your answer with examples from recent news coverage.

4. "It wasn't my story," Everett explains when asked why he is only now looking into the Beachum case. How can news coverage be organized so that stories like Beachum's don't fall through the cracks? Should there be new and different kinds of beats? Collaboration with other institutions? More reporting by teams? Be bold in devising possible solutions.

5. Can a bad person ever be an ethical journalist or vice versa?

6. Describe a situation from your own experience where you had to choose between two prima facie duties. Explain why you found one duty more binding than the other.

FURTHER READING

Dyck, Arthur C. *On Human Care*. Nashville, Tenn.: Abdington, 1977.

Krajicek, David J. *Scooped! Media Miss Real Story on Crime While Chasing Sex, Sleaze, and Celebrities*. New York: Columbia University Press, 1998.

Lambeth, Edmund B. *Committed Journalism*. Bloomington: Indiana University Press, 1986.

Lasch, Christopher. *The Culture of Narcissism*. New York: Norton, 1979.

Ross, W. D. *The Right and the Good*. London: Oxford University Press, 1930.

Sullivan, Roger J. *An Introduction to Kant's Ethics*. Cambridge: Cambridge University Press, 1994.

———. *Morality and the Good Life: A Commentary on Aristotle's* Nicomachean Ethics. Memphis, Tenn.: Memphis University Press, 1977.

9

Network:
Through a Glass Darkly

When it debuted in 1976, *Network* was hailed as a brilliant dark satire whose edge derived from the fact that the film's exaggerations sprung from seeds of truth. *New York Times* reviewer Vincent Canby praised the film but urged his readers not to take it too seriously: "*Network* is not meant to be a realistic movie. . . . It's a roller coaster ride through [screenwriter Paddy] Chayefsky's fantasies as he imagines what television *might* do given the opportunity."

But maybe *Network* was just ahead of its time: In the past quarter-century, given the opportunity, through mergers and government de-regulation, commercial television in the United States has descended from the merely vapid to the truly vulgar. Rupert Murdoch's Fox Network seems actually to have been inspired by the fictional United Broadcasting System (UBS) of *Network*.

Network is an ideal vehicle to explore how the quest for media money can eclipse media ethics. The film depicts, after all, the exploitation of a mentally unbalanced anchorman who vows to commit suicide on the air and then watches his popularity soar as he exhorts television-addicted "humanoids" to seek a life outside the box; the staging of terrorist attacks; an on-air murder; and the transformation of the evening news into a midway freak show complete with a soothsayer. As with *The Wizard of Oz*, however, the truth is to be found behind the curtain—or, in this case, the camera. Because despite UBS's populist rhetoric and sensational shows, two pragmatic objectives—profits and social control—drive the cynical programing it airs to the delight of a mesmerized audience and the horror of anachronistic journalistic purists.

Vulgarity and cynicism drive the plot of *Network*, but the film's central focus is the commodification of human experience, the notion that any facet of human experience—joy, despair, depravity, madness—can be transformed into for-profit entertainment. Television, it often seems, will air anything that produces ratings because ratings produce money. Currently, network television is dominated by "reality" programing that would be quite at home on *Network's* UBS. Shows like *Survivor*, *The Mole*, and *Temptation Island* isolate contestants and set them into psychological conflict under the relentless gaze of the camera. Dramatic tension derives from suspicion, finger-pointing, betrayal, and humiliation in front of a worldwide audience.

The premise and appeal of such programing can be encapsulated in a simple question: How far will people go (or how low will they stoop) to reap the considerable ego and economic rewards the media can confer? Would-be media workers might pose that same question to themselves. *Network*, a scathing depiction of a media universe without moral law, offers one depressingly possible answer: Money talks and morality walks.

THE TUBE IS GOSPEL

The outrageous chain of events that transforms UBS from a struggling but reasonably respectable broadcast network into a electronic madhouse is set into motion by anchorman Howard Beale (Peter Finch). Facing forced retirement because of sagging ratings, Beale has a nervous breakdown on the air and promises to commit suicide during his next broadcast. Given a chance to appear on the air the next night to apologize for his outburst, Beale instead rails against the inanity of television and the stupidity of his audience. Beale blames his breakdown the previous night on the sad fact that he "just ran out of bullshit."

Responsible news executives are appalled at Beale's breakdown and resolve to yank him off the air for good, but entertainment programers at UBS are intrigued. Beale's ranting has generated buzz and high ratings. Programer Diana Christensen (Faye Dunaway) knows a hit when she sees one. She also knows her audience. "The American people are turning sullen," she lectures. "They've been clobbered on all sides by Vietnam, Watergate, the inflation, the depression; they've turned off, shot themselves up and they've fucked themselves limp and nothing helps. The American people want someone to articulate their rage for them."

Beale is merely the centerpiece of UBS's profit-driven "news" division (which falls under the control of entertainment programmers). Under Christensen's ambitious leadership, UBS sets out to trash every notion of journalistic tradition in the pursuit of high ratings and big profits. UBS even goes so far as to form an alliance with a revolutionary group to film its bank robberies—co-opting the Marxist terrorists and transforming them into money-obsessed marketers whose strident idealism withers before the prospect of fame and riches.

Back in the studio, Beale's popularity soars. Far from articulating the audience's rage, he is trying make his viewers *feel* rage at the images and lies that pour out of their televisions. His tirades against the medium and his own company delight his audience and, at first, his bosses, who don't care what Beale says about them as long as people tune in. His lamentation sums up the worst aspects of corporate control of television's cultural and political power:

> The only truth you know is what you get over this tube. Right now, there is an entire goddamned generation that never knew anything that didn't come out of this tube. This tube is gospel, the ultimate revelation. The tube can make or break presidents, popes, prime ministers. This tube is the most awesome, goddamn force in the whole godless world. And woe is us if it ever falls into the hands of the wrong people and that's why it's woe to us [that] this company is now in the hands of CCA, the Communication Corporation of America. And when the twelfth largest company in the world controls the most awesome, goddamn propaganda force in the whole godless world, who knows what shit will be peddled for truth on this network.

"BECAUSE YOU'RE ON TELEVISION, DUMMY"

Beale's exhortations to numb audience members to reject television and reclaim their lives only makes them more loyal viewers, but even good ratings cannot protect Beale from CCA president Arthur

Jensen (Ned Beatty), who becomes perturbed by Beale's increasingly anticapitalist rants—and by his on-air revelation that CCA is about to be swallowed by an even bigger firm, the Arab-controlled World Funding Corporation (WFC).

When Beale's ravings begin to undermine the larger corporate objectives of UBS owners, he is reprogrammed to mouth the capitalist catechism of Jensen (who, he thinks, may just be God). Jensen explains to Beale the true nature of the relationship between the market and the media:

> You have meddled with the forces of nature and you will atone! Am I getting through to you, Mr. Beale? You get up on your little twenty-one-inch screen and howl about America and democracy. There is no America. There is no democracy. There is only IBM and ITT and AT&T and DuPont and Dow and Union Carbide and Exxon—those are the nations of the world today. . . . The world is a college of corporations, inexorably determined by the immutable laws of business, Mr. Beale.

When Beale asks why he has been chosen for the awesome task of making the world safe for global monopoly, Jensen shakes his head and replies, "Because you're on television, dummy."

Ethicist, political economist, and former *Washington Post* editor Ben Bagdikian has spent three decades tracking the accelerating concentration of media conglomerates. As corporate domination expands, the marketplace of ideas contracts. The media, which serve as a vital synapse between the public and the larger political world, "is being reduced to a small number of closed circuits in which the owners of the conduits—newspapers, magazines, broadcast stations, and all other mass media—prefer to use material they own or that tends to suit their economic interests," Bagdikian writes. "It is normal," he adds, "for all large businesses to make serious efforts to influence the news, to avoid embarrassing publicity, and to maximize sympathetic public opinion and government policies. Now they own most of the news media they wish to influence."

Jensen's proposition—and Bagdikian's analysis—neatly frame the ethical questions at the heart of this chapter: Can ethical practices take root and thrive in a media environment driven by the profit motive? Do the corporations that own the media care about ethics? Do individuals working within corporate-dominated media really have the power to behave ethically? Do ongoing trends in media

ownership and programing bode ill for ethical use of a rapidly pro-
liferating mass media that increasingly transcend national boundaries? Exploring possible answers to those question requires a brief
sketch of broadcast journalism's history and of the economic state
of media today.

MURROW'S BOYS

The character of aging news executive Max Schumacher (William
Holden) is caught between two worlds. He is at once a link to a more
ethical broadcasting past and a powerless spectator to an audacious
new world of television "news" shaped by stockholder demands and
finance committees. After an ill-starred fling with ratings-possessed
Diana Christensen, Schumacher—summoning up a vestige of the
integrity he has frittered away at work and at home—delivers a
soliloquy that illuminates the emptiness of both his lover's and his
medium's souls: "It's too late, Diana. There's nothing left in you that
I can live with. You're one of Howard's humanoids. If I stay with you,
I'll be destroyed. Like Howard Beale was destroyed. . . . Like everything that you and the institution of television touch is destroyed.
You're television incarnate, Diana—indifferent to suffering, insensi-
tive to joy."

Old-guard journalists like Schumacher were raised to believe the
press has an almost sacred democratic duty to enlighten citizens regardless of profit. As they console themselves by getting drunk,
Schumacher and Beale reminisce about their glory days with Edward
R. Murrow, the real-life broadcasting pioneer who helped to invent
broadcast news and infuse it with an ethos of responsibility.

At CBS in the 1940s and 1950s (and as the architect of the network's radio news broadcasts before that), Murrow cultivated professionalism in the journalists who worked under him and prodded
his corporate bosses to recognize that television had a moral obligation to devote some of its resources to performing public service. The
Federal Communications Commission (FCC) mandated some service
in exchange for broadcasters' use of the public airwaves and
Murrow's aim was to be sure television journalism honored the spirit,
not the mere letter, of the law. The now quaint-sounding operation
Murrow oversaw at CBS was called the Education Division. When
Schumacher makes Murrow-esque objections to the cheapening of the
UBS news show, he is shouted down by Frank Hackett (Robert

Duvall): "I've had it up to here with your cruddy division and its $33 million deficit. I know that historically news divisions are expected to lose money. But to our minds, this philosophy is a wanton fiscal affront to be resolutely resisted."

Under Hackett's direction, the news division is taken from Schumacher and given to Christensen. She is a programmer, not a journalist, and to her a news show is simply another vehicle to deliver entertainment to the masses and profits to the network, the same as game shows, sitcoms, and soap operas. In fact, her revamped news show—starring "The Mad Prophet of the Airwaves"—possesses elements of all those genres. Christensen's ascension is a direct result of the growing corporate consolidation and diminishing lack of competition in the media. She is given free rein to exploit the news division because UBS is losing ground to its three network competitors. "Mad Prophets" sell, she observes, while real news does not: "The Arabs have decided to jack up the price of oil another 20 percent, the CIA has been caught opening Senator Humphrey's mail, there's a civil war in Beirut, New York City's still facing default, they've finally caught up with Patricia Hearst and the whole front page of the *Daily News* is Howard Beale!"

When Schumacher and Beale recoil at Christensen's strategy, she points out that she is merely building on what they have allowed television to become on their watch. "I watched your six o'clock news today," she says, prior to remaking the program. "It's straight tabloid . . . you had less than a minute of hard national and international news. It was all sex, scandal, brutal crime, sports, children with incurable diseases, and lost puppies. So I don't think I'll listen to any protestations when you're right down on the streets soliciting audiences like the rest of us."

Commercial television stations need audiences and ratings to thrive and the quarterly "sweeps" periods that determine advertising rates indicate that one sure way to get both is to air sensational stories. But how far should broadcast journalists go to lure audiences? Can sensational stories be justified if they attract viewers who also then are exposed to important stories and issues?

In Pittsburgh, CBS-affiliate KDKA regularly wins awards for high-quality journalism but also aired, during the 2001 "sweeps," a nightly segment tracking the progress of a local contestant on the network's *Survivor* show. Does such gimmickry taint the entire newscast? KDKA might answer critics by pointing to fellow CBS affiliate

WBBM in Chicago, where an experiment to purge the nightly newscast of sensationalism, celebrity profiles, and the "if it bleeds it leads" approach to crime coverage was declared a failure after only nine months. Critics hailed the experiment, but Chicago viewers stayed away in droves.

IT'S A SMALL WORLD AFTER ALL

By the time *Network* appeared, the Murrow-era journalists were engaged in fairly open, if futile, combat with MBA-toting media buccaneers who saw in the power of the mass media only the promise of profit and personal advancement. *Network* turns the First Amendment, and the Enlightenment philosophy that underpins it, on their heads. The news programs and workers in *Network* do not exist primarily to inform and empower citizens, but to manipulate their perceptions so that they do not become empowered. Unlike other films in which individuals or organizations behave unethically in the face of standards that implore them not to, many of the characters of *Network* strive to uphold an antiethic.

The ethical crises in *Network*—and in the real media world—stem largely from near-monopoly control of the mass media. Philip Patterson and Lee Wilkins observe, "As media ownership becomes the privilege of the rich, an elite few control an important ingredient of democracy: news. And when the few who own the media view it only as a business, the problem gets worse." The ethical issues embedded in *Network* are far-ranging and complex. They touch individual citizens and communities, individual media workers and entrenched corporate structures, individual government officials and labyrinthine government agencies.

In the United States, a few gigantic corporations own most media outlets and can decide with little interference to use their communications technologies to transmit anything they find suitable, even over the airwaves, which are ostensibly the property of the public. With no one to check their power, these companies can use their media outlets in any way that suits their economic and ideological interests. According to Beale, that almost always means deception and manipulation. "Television is not the truth," he futilely warns his jaded, apathetic audience. "We're in the boredom-killing business . . . you'll never get any truth from us. We'll tell you anything you want to hear. We lie like hell!"

Press critic Bagdikian, in more reasoned language, has reached much the same conclusion as Beale. As media companies merge and acquire one another or become mere cogs in multifaceted financial empires, the marketplace of ideas is being extinguished, Bagdikian warns. In its place is emerging a faux "public forum" full of pseudo-events, homogenized discourse, and corporate propaganda. We have become mute spectators in this new marketplace—indeed, we pay admission for the privilege of listening. Writing in 1997, Bagdikian declared: "In the last five years, a small number of the country's largest industrial corporations has acquired more public communications power—including ownership of the news—than any private businesses have ever before possessed in world history. Nothing in earlier history matches this corporate group's power to penetrate the social landscape. . . . [T]his handful of giants has created what is, in effect, a new communication cartel within the United States."

The rate of media consolidation is accelerating as large corporations merge their traditional information companies with emerging dot.coms. In 1984, Bagdikian identified fifty corporations that largely controlled the media. By 1990, that number had shrunk to twenty-three. In the fifth edition of his ground-breaking *Media Monopoly* in 1997, Bagdikian convincingly argued that power had been consolidated into the hands of roughly ten corporations.

Those ten corporations are by no means strictly American "media" companies. Many are multinational enterprises with interests in banking, weapons, and real estate, much like the WFC in *Network*. For instance, NBC, one of America's largest broadcast networks, is a subsidiary of one of the world's largest manufacturers of armaments—General Electric (GE). Whether they are overseeing missile production or the nightly news, companies like GE expect maximum "bang for the buck"—profits *and* a channel for the dissemination of ideas and information helpful to the parent firm.

An on-going project by Aaron Moore, published on the *Columbia Journalism Review* (*CJR*) Web site, to track media ownership can barely keep pace with industry mergers and acquisitions. A recent merger between Time Warner and America Online—described by *CJR* as "a multi-media monster, the largest corporate merger in U.S. history"—gave the new firm a dominant presence in every single communications medium.

Concentration of media ownership among a few firms has several ramifications. The variety of ideas and perspectives diminishes as fewer entities acquire more channels. In addition, the firms that own most of the media—and therefore the public forum—are quite similar in structure, outlook, and objectives; they use their influence to support legislation favorable to big business in general and to fight government efforts to curtail their influence. In the 1980s, media companies lent editorial support—and provided campaign contributions—to politicians who dismantled decades-old laws limiting the number of television stations one firm could own. Those laws were initially written to prevent monopoly over public discourse. In Bagdikian's words, most of what passes for vital public information is actually an "industrial byproduct."

The sheer number of media outlets available to Americans and citizens of other industrial nations creates an illusion of choice, but when a few corporations own multiple channels of mass communication, real choice is limited and the marketplace of ideas becomes instead a hall of mirrors where the views and agendas of a few big companies are reflected wherever one looks. The power to shape public debate, Bagdikian points out, constitutes added value for astonishingly lucrative media outlets. "Media power is political power . . . [and] most media proprietors show little or no evidence in their programming of any sense of obligation to treat the American audience as members of a Democracy," according to Bagdikian.

News organizations cannot survive without profits, but when they pursue profitability at the expense of responsibility, they lose credibility and fuel public cynicism about journalism and public life. For most of the twentieth century, journalists have tried to preserve their autonomy with an "invisible wall" that separates the newsroom from the baser, money-making operations of the media organization.

The invisible wall supposedly keeps advertising executives, to cite one example, from coercing editors into running stories favorable to advertisers or killing stories that aren't (for an excellent illustration of the "invisible wall" in action, see chapter 2, which discusses the film *Deadline U.S.A.*). But that approach to producing news is changing. Recently, Mark Willes, the chief executive officer of megamedia firm Times Mirror, said he expects the firm's news editors to function like marketers, producing "journalism" carefully tailored to the needs of Times Mirror advertisers and the reader-consumers those advertisers want to reach. Willes, who worked in the cereal industry before being hired to make Times Mirror ship-shape, scoffs at the notion that the newsroom does not answer to a media firm's bottom line: "I have suggested strongly and repeatedly that the people in the newsroom need to know and understand the people in our advertising department. And there has been more than one person who has pointed out the wall between the newsroom and the advertising department. And every time they point it out I get out a bazooka and tell them if they don't take it down, I'm going to blow it up."

Hackett would understand perfectly. The demolition of the invisible wall is at the heart of *Network*. When the wall is gone completely, there is a possibility that there will be nothing left of journalism but marketing. Government censorship of the press is forbidden by the First Amendment, but for most of the twentieth century the government has asserted the right to limit the spread of monopolies. Should government slow, or even undo, the concentration of the media to preserve the diversity of ideas at the heart of our political ideology? Or would such interference in itself violate libertarian principles?

WHO WANTS TO BE A MILLIONAIRE?

Diana Christensen "saves" UBS by stealing what is left of its soul. As befits a person who seems to have been wholly raised by television, she cannot break out of the box she lives in. She sees television-style melodrama everywhere and reacts to others as if she and they are characters in a miniseries. "All I want out of life is a thirty share and a twenty rating!" she declares. She has given herself wholly over to her work and the shallow pursuit of profits—and by that particular criteria, she has been quite successful.

A critical—and legitimate—concern among ethical young people entering the media is whether they can make a living while staying true to their values. What can one person—particularly one at the bottom of the corporate food chain—do to influence policies within his or her organization? What can one person do—short of giving up a job and possibly a career—to protest or even simply resist directives that violate his or her values? There are, obviously, no easy answers. But there are scales on which individuals might weigh their choices in a high-pressure profession fraught with ethical land mines. On one side of the scale is the denial of individual responsibility; on the other is unswerving obligation to live strictly within principles one deems ethical. Some points on the ethical continuum are:

I Was Only Following Orders

This defense was invoked by Nazi functionaries at the Nuremberg war crimes tribunal after World War II. Since they had been given direct orders by their country's leaders to murder, midlevel officers argued, they should not be held personally responsible for their actions—which collectively amounted to genocide. The tribunal rejected this argument, reasoning that, in a world of hierarchies, validating such an excuse would make it impossible to hold individuals accountable for anything. Media employees cannot be court-martialed or shot for refusing to carry out orders, but they can be fired, demoted, or otherwise punished. Outright disobedience carries consequences in the corporate world.

An employee who takes the "I was only following orders" approach eludes responsibility in a wholly superficial way. We all know in our hearts that we are responsible for our own actions. And yet the lament that "the boss made me do it" is common among media workers. For instance, a camera crew in the early 1980s filmed a man who set fire to himself after notifying the television station. The crew was sent to get footage, so it got footage. Once they got enough footage, crew members doused the man, who suffered extensive third-degree burns. Because the man staged his immolation for the cameras, only the most twisted interpretation of news values could be used to justify such an act.

People Get the Kind of Media They Deserve

Cynicism is an understandable response to untenable circumstances. Media workers who help create programs or stories that are phony, tasteless, or morally wormy often shrug off responsibility by claiming they are only giving the audience what the audience wants. Besides, cynics argue, if they don't carry out their company's orders, someone else will.

The cynical approach is also, at heart, dishonest and evasive. Surrender to cynicism forecloses the possibility of ever acting positively. In truth, people get the kind of media that media companies give them. Individuals and groups committed to the creation of quality programming sometimes manage to produce quality programming even at ethically questionable companies. The Internet, while undergoing rapid commercialization, does offer citizens the chance to slip by the gatekeepers to construct their own news agenda and to gain access to sources and points of view that are simply not available through traditional media.

Take This Job and Shove It

Cognitive psychology has identified several personality types, including one called "the noble self." A person with a noble self sees any deviation from his or her principles as an unacceptable compromise. Such a rigid approach to work and ethics—not to mention life— may indeed preserve one's values, but it also diminishes the possibility for doing good. If ethical people abandon the media to the Diana Christensens of the world, the media would be in much worse shape than it now is. Working within an organization to promote ethics and find creative solutions to ethical dilemmas is a more rational course. The fact is that short of joining communes or retreating to the deep forests as Ted Kaczynski, the Unabomber, did, prospective American media workers are going to toil in a capitalist economic system that often pits profits against personal values or professional expectations; such clashes are a reality in every economic and political system.

I Prefer Not To

Bartleby, the harried scrivener in the story by Herman Melville, refuses to do a task he finds distasteful; in fact, he refuses to even explain why he finds it so. A morally mature person knows he or she has an obligation to refuse repugnant directives, no matter the cost. But not all situations are as clear-cut as, say, deciding whether news values require one to film a man who wants to set himself afire on television. An individual might work at a television station that runs some good programs and some questionable ones. A reporter might work at a paper that does some useful investigation, but also turns over huge swathes of its news hole to the coverage of celebrities.

It is wise policy to explain one's motives for refusing to carry out a task—and to be ready with an acceptable alternative. On the one hand, a reporter might reluctantly agree to cover a story he or she considers frivolous. He or she might also attempt to initiate a policy discussion about how to decide what is newsworthy. On the other hand, a reporter might refuse outright to knowingly put untrue information into a story, knowing that the refusal might lead to disciplinary action or, perhaps, a reconsideration of the order itself. Reporters who have been troubled by the practices of their publications have been known to leak information about an ethical breach to a competitor or professional journal, or remove their bylines from the stories they file.

When Pulitzer Prize–winning *New York Newsday* columnist Jimmy Breslin launched an obscene and racist tirade at an Asian colleague, outraged *Newsday* staffers leaked news of the incident to competitors; once their stories broke, Breslin was reprimanded and suspended. Faced with competing loyalties—their sense of justice and decency versus their loyalty to *Newsday*—the whistle-blowers honored universal values. In the end, *Newsday* management's punishment of Breslin, who otherwise has had an exemplary career, served to restore the respect of its journalists.

THE BIG PICTURE

In the end, neither media workers nor any other workers are trapped in an air-tight dichotomy. Some media companies *are* more responsible than others. Some company policies *can* be challenged and modified or overturned. Professional standards *do* sometimes successfully give individual media workers the backup they need to assert their values. Professional criticism, like that found in the *CJR* or at Salon.com, *do* expose media wrongdoing and create embarrassing pressure to rectify it. Nor must entry- or midlevel media workers assume all ethical responsibility for their profession. A commitment to ethics has to start at the top of the organizational chart. In recent decades, some entrepreneurs have advocated "doing well by doing good" and adopted tough ethical standards they expect themselves and their subordinates to live up to. In addition, laws and regulations aimed at curbing sexual harassment and racial discrimination have fostered more humane working conditions.

And the audience, certainly, is not free of ethical responsibility for the conditions depicted in *Network* and pervasive in today's media. When academics, media workers, corporate officials, or government agents assume that the public is not to be trusted with decisions that affect the public forum, they are helping to foster the very cynicism they claim to deplore and undermining the very philosophical principles many claim to hold dear. Children spend upwards of thirty hours a week in front of the television and countless hours Web surfing or playing computer games. Allowing one's children such immersion is probably in itself unethical, but parents who abdicate responsibility for monitoring their children's media usage are, in essence, giving amoral programmers like Christensen the opportunity to shape their children's sense of right and wrong. Likewise, educators who do nothing to encourage media literacy or teach their charges some of the grammars of the media have failed in their mission to help them become critical thinkers.

Ethical models explored in detail elsewhere in this book can help individuals navigate the ethical shoals that will inevitably confront them—including concentrated ownership of the media. Aristotle suggested that within every ethical dilemma there is a mean, or middle way, open to individuals and, by implication, to professions and industries. Rather than compromising their values completely to attain employment or advancement, media workers can find creative compromises that honor their values and help them advance in their profession without doing public harm.

Despite the rapid consolidation of the media, there remain independently owned media firms and large media companies that set their course according to a moral, as well as a financial, compass. And the Internet—in the early stages of being digested by global conglomerates—also offers lucrative outlets for independent voices. *Network*, intended as a cautionary tale, has in many respects proved prophetic. But there remain ethical media organizations, executives, managers, and front-line workers. Young people who enter the media have to decide whether they are willing to do the hard ethical work and make the hard ethical choices it takes to join them.

FINE TUNING

Media critics grapple with how to slow the growth of media consolidation and the potential for social control it represents. Few would seriously advocate abrogating the First Amendment, but when global conglomerates use the right of free speech to monopolize speech, the spirit of the document has obviously been subverted.

At the most basic level, many ethicists and media critics would like to revive the Hutchins Commission Report on the Freedom of the Press (detailed in chapter 2), which implored media owners to exercise responsibility and provide the public with vital information whether it suits corporate interests or not.

Media critics and professional organizations, such as the SPJ, urge the revival of press councils that hear citizen complaints about media coverage. The recommendations of those councils, which were briefly in vogue during the 1960s and 1970s, were not binding, but their very existence proved an annoyance to publishers who were called to task for actions in the public forum.

Broadcasting has always fallen under government regulation because the airwaves broadcasters use are considered a scarce natural resource and therefore public property. Networks and broadcast stations are granted licenses to use the airwaves. Prior to the 1980s, responsible use of those airwaves was a condition of receiving and keeping a license. The federal "Fairness Doctrine" required stations to give air time, for example, to allow those with divergent political views to respond to political statements made by the station or its favored officials and candidates. In addition, the FCC imposed ownership limits on individual companies to ensure that no one company could establish a local or national media monopoly. A revival of those rules would not end corporate dominance of the media, but it would allow greater choice between corporate viewpoints.

The federal government originally asserted control of the airwaves to prevent signal chaos, but, as a result, only the biggest firms can afford to buy broadcast licenses. Using their influence, these firms fight every effort to license low-power broadcast outlets that serve small areas or communities with no interference with the signals of large broadcasters. Small stations might, however, siphon off potential audience members, who would then be unavailable to hear the commercials that other firms pay dearly to broadcast.

Heavy-handed government control of the media would be undesirable and would run afoul of the First Amendment. But taking a near-total hands-off approach, as the government does now, simply allows for corporate control of the public forum. A middle way might be for the government—which is, in theory at least, the representative of the citizenry—to act as an honest broker and design policies that maintain press freedom while ensuring the free flow of ideas vital to democracy.

FADE TO BLACK

After Max Schumacher falls for Diana Christensen and deserts his wife to take up with her, he discovers that life in a twenty-one-inch world is too confining for someone with real feelings and thoughts. Christensen talks passionately about programing while she and Schumacher make love and frustrates his every attempt at meaningful conversation by framing the topic in terms of television genre. Even their relationship is a disposable script. "Well, Max, here we are," she says after he has moved in with her, "middle-aged man reaffirming his manhood, and a terrified young woman with a father complex. What kind of script do you think we can make out of this?"

Critics like Neil Postman and Neal Gabler have warned that mass entertainment—especially television—is so pervasive and powerful that it has become the template for human behavior rather than a reflection of it. In his book *Life the Movie: How Entertainment Conquered Reality*, Gabler asserts that people gauge the reality of their lives by how closely their lives resemble television. Postman laments that we are "amusing ourselves to death."

The bleak picture of the media painted by *Network* is manifest daily on television, in theaters, and on the Internet. Standards of taste and moral sense have undoubtedly decayed. And yet, the box is only powerful if we turn it on. Unwatched shows perish. Individuals can and do make choices about what programs they will support, but with diversity of ownership shrinking there are few opportunities to make their perspectives heard—or to demand that they be represented in the media. The companies that control the media invoke First Amendment rights when government agencies threaten to put a brake on media consolidation or take steps to diversify ownership or programing. It's unlikely, however, that the framers of the Constitution intended the First Amendment to ensure that monopolies can assert complete control over the public forum.

In the absence of meaningful action on the part of citizens and their elected representatives to slow the rate of media consolidation, Howard Beale's scathing description of the corporate media's ultimate effects, and the remedy he proposes to his faithful audience, continue to resonate: "You do whatever the tube tells you. You dress like the tube, you eat like the tube, you raise your children like the tube. You even think like the tube. This is mass madness, you maniacs. In God's name, you people are the real thing. We are the illusion. So turn off your televisions. Turn them off and leave them off."

QUESTIONS TO CONSIDER

1. To what extent do you think *Network* reflects the reality of the American media and cultural landscape? Is it simply a sly fantasy, as critic Vincent Canby said when it was released? Or does it accurately reflect the mindset that produces our television shows and other media products?

2. Which do you feel poses a greater threat to freedom of expres-

sion in the United States, the government or the corporate media? Why?

3. Why *do* people watch so many "lousy" programs on television. Are they stupid sheep, as UBS programers seem to think? What options are open to individual audience members who want to voice their views in the public forum?

4. At the national level, what actions by government agencies, corporations, citizens' groups, or some combination of the three might serve to reverse monopoly control of the press and open the public forum to a greater diversity of viewpoints?

5. At the local level, what actions by government agencies (school boards, city councils, and so on) media outlets, and citizens groups might elevate the level of public discourse in your community? At the individual level, what actions could you take to raise the level of public discourse in your role as a citizen, audience member, student, or media worker?

6. Is it possible to infuse the media job you might hold someday with a sense of ethics? What actions, for instance, might you take in your first job at a television station, advertising agency, or newspaper that would contribute to the ethical atmosphere of your workplace?

FURTHER READING

Bagdikian, Ben. *The Media Monopoly*. 5th ed. Boston: Beacon, 1997.

Canby, Vincent. "A Surreal Attack on American Life." *New York Times*, 28 November 1976, D-17.

Cloud, Stanley, and Lynne Olson. *The Murrow Boys: Pioneers on the Front Lines of Broadcast Journalism*. Boston: Houghton Mifflin, 1996.

Dillon, Mike. "Jimmy Breslin." In *New Journalists: Dictionary of Literary Biography*, ed. Arthur Kaul. Detroit, Mich.: Bruccoli Clark Layman/ Gale Research, 1997.

Gabler, Neal. *Life the Movie: How Entertainment Conquered Reality*. New York: Knopf, 1998.

Hickey, Neil. "Chicago Experiment—Why It Failed." *Columbia Journalism Review* (January–February 2001).

Iggers, Jeremy. "Get Me Rewrite." *Utne Reader* (September–October 1997): 46.

Lewis, Charles. "Media Money: How Corporate Spending Blocked Political Ad Reform and Other Stories of Influence." *Columbia Journalism Review* (May–June 2000).

Moore, Aaron. "Who Owns What: *CJR*'s Web Guide to What the Major Media Companies Own." *Columbia Journalism Review*, October 22, 2001.

Owen, Rob, and Barbara Vancheri. "TV Stations Often Promise More Than They Deliver When Playing the Promotional Ratings Game." *Pittsburgh Post-Gazette*, 22 February 2001, E-1.

Patterson, Philip, and Lee Wilkins, ed. *Media Ethics: Issues and Cases*. 2nd ed. Madison, Wis.: Brown and Benchmark, 1994.

Postman, Neil. *Amusing Ourselves to Death: Public Discourse in the Age of Show Business*. New York: Viking, 1985.

Postman, Neil, and Steve Powers. *How to Watch TV News*. New York: Penguin, 1992.

Tuchman, Gaye. *Making News: A Study in the Construction of Reality*. New York: The Free Press, 1978.

10

The Rock:
The Ethics of
Entertainment Violence

Flames leap from the steel-blue muzzles of automatic rifles. Bullets punch big, ugly holes in flesh. Wounds spout gobs of blood. The air fills with a demented chorus of screams, curses, sighs, and grunts. Men throw up their arms and die; claw at their throats and die; grab their midsections and die. In just a few apocalyptic moments, the dead outnumber the living.

News footage of the latest genocidal war in Eastern Europe? A child's nightmare? An overheated vision of hell? Hardly. It is a scene from the hit action movie *The Rock* and a typical example of entertainment violence.

George Gerbner, one of the first to study the psychological and social effects of violent television programing, defines entertainment violence as "the overt, physical demonstration of power that hurts or kills." Today entertainment violence isn't only more graphic than ever before, but also more readily available. At any hour of the day or night, it can be viewed on cable TV, the Internet, computer games, or videotapes.

The grisly evolution of entertainment violence is summed up by John Seabrook in his book *Nobrow: The Culture of Marketing—the Marketing of Culture*. Seabrook remembers playing as a teenager in the early 1980s a video game called Missile Command, where the object was to try to save the world. He notes that the "first-person shooter" games that are now popular have names like Doom and Quake, and the best you can hope for is to save yourself. Players, who see through the eyes of a killer holding a gun or other weapon, are rewarded for slashing, gouging, and shooting opponents.

Is the increase in entertainment violence cause for alarm? According to national opinion polls, the American public believes so. An Associated Press survey found that 82 percent of the public consider movies too violent, while a *Los Angeles Times* survey found that the same percentage think the amount of violence in movies is harmful to society. In another survey, 76 percent of respondents asserted that media portrayals of violence desensitizes people; 71 percent, that the media convey the message that "violence is fun and acceptable"; and 75 percent, that media violence inspires children and adolescents to real violence.

Public anxiety about the effects of entertainment violence, particularly on young people, has been heightened by recent shootings at schools in one all-American community after another—Pearl, Mississippi; Paducah, Kentucky; Littleton, Colorado; Conyers, Georgia; Santana, California. Some claim that the common thread in these tragedies isn't lax gun laws or a superabundance of household guns, but a popular culture that exalts violence. "Only the most jaded nihilist," film critic Michael Medved writes, "could take comfort from a situation in which bloody scenes deemed unbearably disturbing by past generations are now accepted as an integral element of the popular culture. The higher level of tolerance for media violence may even promote the acceptance of the blood-curdling cruelty we experience with increasing frequency in our own homes and communities."

Politicians with something to prove to voters have also cast a critical eye on the media. In a 1995 speech in Los Angeles, home of the entertainment industry, Republican presidential candidate Bob Dole declared: "Movies and music do not make children into murderers. But a numbing exposure to graphic violence and immorality does steal away innocence, smothering our instinct for outrage. We have reached the point where our popular culture threatens to undermine our character as a nation." Four years later, after the killings at Columbine High School in Littleton, there were Senate hearings and a White House summit on entertainment violence, though little actual change.

While not even Medved or Dole was ready to argue that entertainment violence directly causes violent behavior, evidence suggests that it may be a significant contributing factor. In 2000 the FBI released an "offender profile" based on information gathered from six school shootings and intended to help identify violence-prone students. The profile included spending forty hours or more a week viewing violent video entertainment.

Research on media violence—and there have been approximately three thousand studies conducted since the 1960s—has overwhelmingly found that repeated exposure to violent programming poses mental health risks, particularly to children and adolescents. Most of the studies have examined television, but, as family psychologist Madeline Levine points out, "many of the findings are equally applicable to movies, which regularly feature far more brutal and graphic depictions of violence than either cable or broadcast television."

The American Psychological Association's 1993 report "Violence and Youth: Psychology's Response" reviewed the existing research on media violence. According to the report, the consumption of violent material has four long-term effects:

1. Increased fearfulness
2. Increased desensitization to violence and victims of violence
3. Increased appetite for more violence in entertainment and real life
4. Increased aggressiveness

The first two effects are most often linked to the viewing of media violence generally, including crime-loving, death-saturated newscasts; the latter two are linked to the viewing of entertainment violence in particular.

Viewers may disagree as to just how entertaining *The Rock* is, but they would have to agree that it is exceedingly violent. For two hours and twenty minutes, the film careens from one hard-core action sequence to another. The audience is pounded by gory close-ups of nerve gas eating through skin, entry wounds spewing blood, and mangled bodies twitching in death.

Not everyone is concerned about the negative effects of such graphic violence—or is even convinced that any negative effects exist. English professor Craig Fischer wrote an open letter in reply to Dole's speech, claiming that denunciations of violent entertainment were misguided and simplistic. "I don't believe we can ever adequately understand media effects on audiences," Fischer said, "since response depends so heavily on the subjectivities of each spectator, who—due to race, class, gender, intellectual training, conditions of reception, notions of pleasure, and a thousand other personal factors—may or may not be predisposed to consider a film or TV show . . . 'capable of riling up a postal worker enough to go out and open fire at McDonalds.'" John Woo, a director whose stylish, hyperviolent films have earned him the nicknames "the poet of spilled blood" and "the Mozart of mayhem," expresses similar confidence in audiences' ability to withstand the sight of cinematic carnage. "Violence in real life is horrid, frightening," he says. "Movies are fake, not real. People know that movies are not real."

So is entertainment violence an issue or not? And if it is an issue, how can it best be addressed? Through government control? Self-regulation by the entertainment industry? Parental supervision of young viewers? In an era when most children spend approximately twenty-five hours each week watching television, and television depicts approximately twenty acts of violence each hour, these are questions that need answering. The search for answers starts us climbing up *The Rock*.

LIKE A ROCK

Released in the summer of 1996, *The Rock* today ranks sixtieth in all-time box-office receipts, with a domestic gross of $134 million and a foreign gross of $196.4 million, for a total gross of $330.4 million. Media analyst George Gerbner cites a lucrative foreign market as one reason for the proliferation of violent entertainment despite polls indicating Americans would prefer other kinds of films and television shows. "Everyone understands an action movie," he quotes a Hollywood producer as saying. "If I tell a joke, you may not get it, but if a bullet goes through the window, we all know how to hit the floor, no matter the language." Ethically, of course, profitability is no excuse for doing harm (and the vast majority of research insists that entertainment violence is harmful). As German cleric Wolfgang Huber notes, "Just because there is a market for treating living things with contempt is not a justification for sharing this contempt or even profiting from it."

The Rock has a cartoonish plot that, in the retelling, may seem to treat the audience's intelligence with contempt. A much-decorated but deranged General Francis X. Hummel (Ed Harris) seizes the famous former prison on Alcatraz Island—the "Rock" of the title—with a band of elite troops and threatens to fire missiles armed with VX nerve gas at San Francisco unless his demands are met. Just so the audience knows exactly how hideous the effects of the nerve gas are, the film early on showcases one of the bad guys being accidentally exposed to the stuff. His face blisters and melts like a marshmallow in a microwave.

Lawrence Kasdan, the writer-director of such hit films of the 1980s as *The Big Chill* and *Silverado*, might have had *The Rock* in mind while criticizing the meretriciousness of contemporary Hollywood films. "Narrative structure doesn't exist," he complains. "All that matters is what's going to happen in the next ten minutes to keep the audience interested. There's no faith in the audience. They can't have the story happen fast enough." And, in fact, hardly a minute goes by in *The Rock* without another gun battle or giant fireball or car chase erupting.

Washington orders a team of U.S. Navy Seals to assault the prison fortress, rescue eighty-one tourists being held hostage, and disarm the missiles. Reluctantly accompanying the attack force are the film's heroes, Patrick Mason (Sean Connery), a former British secret agent and the only man to ever escape from Alcatraz, and Stanley Goodspeed (Nicolas Cage), an FBI chemist. Mason is what is known in folklore studies as "a prowess hero," a Herculean figure who uses strength and combat skills to succeed, while Goodspeed is more "a trickster hero," depending on esoteric knowledge and quick wits to survive. After the Seals are massacred in a prolonged shoot-out, their bodies twisting and falling in a slow-motion ballet of death, this odd couple must complete the rescue mission amid further violence and slaughter—interspersed, naturally, with a few laughs.

Many critics were blown away by *The Rock*. Roger Ebert of the *Chicago Sun-Times* gave the film a big thumbs-up, calling it "a first-rate, slam-bang action thriller with a lot of style and no little humor." *Time* magazine's Richard Corliss said *The Rock* was "[s]lick, brutal and almost human," and as if these were terms of praise, recommended it over *Mission: Impossible*, a Tom Cruise vehicle then also playing at multiplexes. Peter Stack, apparently catching a serious case of hyperbole from the over-the-top film, raved in the *San Francisco Chronicle* that *The Rock* was "a raucous, in-your-face, commando-style action thriller," "a blast of a movie," and a "heavy-metal cinematic event." Andrew Douglas simply described it on Roughcut.com as "a thrilling and witty action picture that gives plenty of bang for the summer buck."

But is there not something strange in critics finding a gorefest like *The Rock* "highly entertaining" and just the sort of thing to recommend to the public? Sissela Bok notes in her book *Mayhem: Violence As Public Entertainment* that film critics may be "the most heavily exposed consumers" of entertainment violence, along with children, invalids, and prisoners, and that a risk of their heavy exposure is desensitization, a kind of numbness. "The trouble is," Bok adds, "that the less empathy critics come to be able to muster for suffering, the more difficult it is for them to serve the needs of viewers less hardened than themselves."

A few critics have openly worried about this deadening of emotion. In a 1997 article in *Esquire* titled "A Gore Phobia," David Thomson recounts gruesome moments from several recent films—including "a floor-level shot of a heavy glass tabletop embedded in a man's head, the joint sealed with bubbling blood"—then suggests that "many of us (especially movie buffs) have become blase about these appalling sights: that's why the movies must strive even harder to shock us. We see, but don't always register the pain or the horror." Pauline Kael, a longtime film critic for the *New Yorker*, sounded even bleaker in her evaluation of entertainment violence:

> It's the emotionlessness of so many violent movies that I'm anxious about, not the rare violent movies (*Bonnie and Clyde*, *The Godfather*, *Mean Streets*) that make us care about characters and what happens to them. A violent movie that intensifies our experience of violence is very different from a movie in which acts of violence are perfunctory. I'm only guessing, and maybe this emotionlessness means little, but, if I can trust my instincts at all, there's something deeply wrong about anyone's taking for granted the dissociation that this carnage without emotion represents.

The uneasiness Kael felt while viewing most violent films wasn't unlike the uneasiness the philosopher Seneca felt while contemplating gladiatorial combat and other violent entertainment in ancient Rome. Seneca claimed that the spectacle of gladiators fighting to the death or of criminals being thrown to the lions brutalized and desensitized Romans—made them *"crudelior et inhumanior"* ("more cruel and more inhumane"). Their pleasure in watching violence not only undercut what he took to be the central task of life—to grow in nobility of spirit, understanding, and self-control—but also actually reversed the development. It destroyed *humanitas*, which Bok translates as "the respectful kindness that characterizes persons who have learned how to be fully human among other humans."

If ethics is based on empathy—that is, the ability to feel with and for others—then the desensitization associated with heavy exposure to media violence may erode the very basis of ethics. "We are losing our awareness of what it means to be human," states Levine, "as we become less responsive to human suffering. Although we may never engage in violent acts or endorse violence ourselves, we may not dislike it nearly as much as we should." In fact, the appetite for more frequent and graphic violence increases with the degree of desensitization. Director Alan Pakula compares film violence to eating salt: "The more you eat, the more you need to eat to taste it at all." This is apparently why body counts always rise in the sequels to action films. The first *Die Hard* film had 18 deaths, and the second, 264; the first *Robocop* film had 32 deaths, the second, 81.

Media violence also takes its toll on viewers in the form of increased fear. Studies have found, for example, that heavy TV viewers are more likely than light viewers to overestimate their chances of becoming a victim of violence; to believe that their neighborhoods are unsafe; to state that crime is rising despite facts to the contrary; and to regard the world as hostile and gloomy—a cluster of responses Gerbner dubs the "mean world syndrome." Sister Elizabeth Thoman, executive director of the Center for Media Literacy in Los Angeles, points out that the syndrome shows up in all sorts of socially toxic ways, from mistrust of others to handguns for personal protection, from barred doors to support for the death penalty.

The philosophers ask: What does it mean to be human? Bok would say it means resisting the effects of media violence—desensitization, appetite, fear, and aggression—and developing instead empathy, self-control, and a respect for life, all characteristics that contribute to "human thriving." But the slickness with which violence is often depicted in the media today may make resistance difficult, even futile.

ROCK OF AGES

Not all depictions of violence are harmful. Spectacularly violent acts—matricide, patricide, fratricide, infanticide—erupt in the Bible, fairy tales, Greek mythology, and Shakespeare's tragedies. What separates these classic depictions from those of today is that today's are glib and without substance, aiming merely to entertain. Entertainment violence may be graphic, but it sheds little light on the role or consequences of violence in the real world. "This sleight of hand," Gerbner writes, "robs us of the tragic sense of life necessary for compassion."

According to the National Television Violence Study, a major undertaking by researchers at the universities of North Carolina, Wisconsin, Texas, and California, the risk of viewers becoming desensitized, aggressive, or fearful is strongly influenced by the way in which violence is depicted. The study identified nine factors that contribute to the effects of entertainment violence on viewers:

1. Perpetrator: If a character perceived as "good" is perpetrating the violence, viewers might imitate the violent behavior. If the character is perceived as evil, viewers might become more fearful of others.

2. Victim: Viewers who are attracted to or identify with a victim of violence are likely to experience increased anxiety and apprehension.

3. Reason: When violence is seen as justified (the hero must kill the villain to save the world), the aggressive tendencies of viewers increase. When violence is seen as unjustified (a robber shoots a store clerk), their aggressive tendencies decrease.

4. Weapons: The presence of weapons can stimulate aggressive thoughts and actions in viewers and influence the interpretation of neutral events as possibly threatening.

5. Prolonged exposure: Repeated exposure to media violence brings about detachment and numbing. The overall effect can be the acceptance of violence as a way to solve problems.

6. Realism: The more realistic a violent act, the more likely it is to elicit aggressive behavior from viewers.

7. Rewards and punishments: Violence that is rewarded or not punished increases the risk of viewers learning aggressive behavior. Violence that is punished decreases that risk.

8. Consequences: Depictions of pain and suffering inhibit aggressive behavior, while depictions of violence as swift, painless, and effective increase aggression.

9. Humor: When combined with violence, humor may trivialize a viewer's perception of violence and its consequences.

Some of these factors clearly apply to *The Rock*. Reviews, for example, praised the film's humor. In one scene, Mason, the former secret agent, steals a Humvee and leads authorities on a delirious chase up and down the steep streets of San Francisco. Pursued and pursuers smash through storefronts, a construction site, a fruit-and-vegetable stand, utility poles, a truckload of water jugs, and a cable car. Mason is rather wry about the damage he causes. After a police car spins out of control, slams into a wall, and explodes, he glances back over his shoulder and quips, "Hope you're insured."

Medved criticizes the entertainment industry's "tendency to make mayhem a subject of mirth." He cites a scene from *Predator* (1987) in which Arnold Schwarzenegger nails a bad guy to a tree with a machete, then urges the bleeding victim to "stick around." Gerbner also objects to this interweaving of comedy and carnage in action films, terming it "happy violence." Both he and Medved assert that having heroes crack one-liners while others die agonizing deaths trivializes the real-world consequences of violence—the physical handicaps, financial expense, and emotional suffering. As if in proof, audiences increasingly respond to scenes of blood and pain not with sympathy, but with sadistic laughter. A twelve-year-old girl, interviewed after a matinee of Schwarzenegger's *Total Recall* (1990), told *Entertainment Weekly*: "I can't say that it's violent, really. It's pretty funny to see people getting shot in the head."

What about to see them get blown up by bombs, impaled by missiles, or melted by nerve gas? The presence of weapons is another factor said to contribute to the effects of entertainment violence on viewers. *The Rock*, which was made with the cooperation of the U.S. armed services, features a vast array of weapons and other military hardware. Just a partial list includes attack helicopters, jet fighters, night-vision goggles, tranquilizer darts, mobile missile launchers, flak vests, incendiaries, and machine guns of apparently every size, shape, and caliber.

But it isn't only the presence of weapons that matters; the way in which the weapons are presented matters, too. In *The Rock*, the camera lingers on the guided missiles pointed at San Francisco, seeming to adoringly stroke the glossy metal skin of their shafts. The film is shot in a style that might be termed "martial porn." Director Michael

Bay is at least as interested in showing off the high-tech machinery of modern war as in exploring character or telling a coherent story. He treats viewers to recurrent sequences of monster helicopters beating the air like winged dragons; of men, all muscle and sweat and concentration, hunting each other with the latest detection devices; of gun muzzles spitting out bright seeds of flame. This is just the sort of sado-chic glamorization of weapons that the National Television Violence Study found promotes violence.

The study also found that violence by good guys is more likely than violence by bad guys to encourage aggressive behavior among viewers. Although initially Goodspeed, the nerdy FBI scientist, is "barely aware he owns a service revolver," he becomes adept at violence over the course of the film. In one particularly gory scene, he stuffs a glowing green ball of nerve gas into the mouth of a bad guy, who then implodes.

As gruesome as this good guy violence can get—Mason stabs one bad guy right through the throat—it is justifiable within the context. Not only are the good guys trying to save San Francisco, but also most of the bad guys in the film are really bad. They deserve to be clobbered by the good guys for mutinying against the government, wanting to execute innocent hostages, and threatening to launch chemical warheads. And remember another finding of the National Television Violence Study: When violence is depicted as justified, the aggressive tendencies of viewers increase.

Given what research on entertainment violence has shown, does society have a stake in controlling depictions of violence like those in *The Rock*? Or are the effects of censorship even worse than the effects of entertainment violence? Or perhaps entertainment violence, in its denial of human dignity and desensitization of the human heart, is itself a form of censorship.

ROCKIN' IN THE FREE WORLD

The United States, where the First Amendment has protected freedom of expression for more than two hundred years, is the least censored society in the world. Even some of the harshest critics of entertainment violence hold firmly to First Amendment principles. For example, Gerbner argues, "More freedom from violent and other inequitable and intimidating formulas, not more censorship, is the effective and acceptable way to . . . reduce television violence to its legitimate role and proportion." A majority of Americans agree. Polls show that despite their concern over sex and violence in entertainment, nearly twice as many people—53 percent to 29 percent—feel government restrictions on the entertainment industry would pose a greater danger than the production of sexual or violent material.

Does this mean we must just learn to live with the harmful effects of entertainment violence? Not necessarily. Several alternatives lie between a laissez-faire approach to entertainment violence and government censorship, between not intervening at all and intervening too much. The most commonly mentioned are industry self-regulation, the V-chip, and media literacy.

Under pressure from the public and theater owners, the film industry adopted a ratings system in 1968. The television industry only recently followed suit, with broadcasters deciding in 1996 to rate their own programs before the government stepped in and did it for them. Film ratings range from G (general audience), PG (parental guidance suggested), and PG-13 (parental guidance strongly suggested for children under thirteen) up to R (under seventeen requires accompanying parent or adult) and NC-17 (no one under seventeen admitted). Television ratings are even more age-specific.

Despite their complicated nomenclature, rating systems are supposed to inform parents. Jack Valenti, president of the Motion Picture Association of America (MPAA) and architect of the film ratings system, explains that the MPAA is concerned with finding out what "most American parents will think about film content." It employs a board of seven Los Angeles–area parents full-time for this purpose. Studios and producers voluntarily submit films to the board, which rates each on the basis of theme, language, nudity, sex, drug use, and violence. A film's MPAA rating appears in ads and reviews. Unsubmitted films—usually foreign or independent productions—are advertised as unrated and may be hard to market.

Some experts criticize the MPAA ratings system for reflecting what is offensive to parents rather than what poses a risk to children. Barbara J. Wilson, a professor of communication at the University of California, Santa Barbara, says film ratings have "tended to be restrictive on sexual content, but lenient on violence." She asserts that depictions of violence are rated according to faulty criteria.

The MPAA ratings are based primarily on the amount and explicitness of violence in films. But, Wilson points out, "perhaps more important than the sheer volume of violent actions . . . is the way in which even a small amount of violence is portrayed." As discussed earlier, research has shown that contextual features—which characters perpetrate violence, why they do, and whether they do it with humor—contribute to harmful effects on viewers. The fact that the good guys in films like *The Rock* commit just as much mayhem as the bad guys can, for example, activate violent thoughts and behaviors. And while *The Rock* did receive an R rating, it was for containing "sexual situations, profanity, major violence and graphic reactions to nerve gas," not for depicting violence as beneficial and justified or the violent as attractively witty.

Wilson also questions the assumption, implicit in the current ratings categories, that the younger the viewer, the greater the risk of harmful effects occurring. She cites research findings that certain violent acts, such as those depicted with a degree of realism and featuring preteen or teen characters, may pose a greater risk to older children. "Preteen viewers, who are typically interested in motives and searching for role models," she says, "might be more inclined to imitate the behaviors seen than a younger child who doesn't yet grasp the complexity of how motivation affects action."

Although admitting that ratings reform is far from easy, Wilson doesn't think it is impossible. She suggests that ratings systems be crafted in light of social science research on the effects of entertainment violence. Others believe, however, that the solution lies with technology.

The same year TV executives vowed to develop a ratings system, the Telecommunications Act of 1996 mandated that the V-chip be included in all new TV sets. The V-chip—the "V" stands for violence—works in conjunction with ratings, both the TV Parental Guidelines and the MPAA ratings (used on any unedited films shown on premium cable channels). The rating that flashes on the screen during the first fifteen seconds of a show transmits an electronic identification signal. All TV sets with the V-chip can receive and decode the signal. By programing a V-chip TV set to block selected signals, parents can prevent children from seeing shows that carry a rating indicating violent or sexual content.

But it isn't possible to filter out all violence. Some shows with violence—such as a documentary on Nazi death camps or a Road Runner cartoon—will not routinely be blocked by the V-chip. In addition, news and sports are exempt, even though research has found that newscasts play as large a role in desensitization and the "mean world syndrome" as entertainment violence does.

Ratings systems, whether used alone or in combination with the V-chip, can't entirely protect children from objectionable material. What ratings and the V-chip can do is increase viewer autonomy. Ratings warn viewers about the nature of a film or TV show. The V-chip empowers them to act on the warning.

This is democracy at work—or is it? Just because people have the opportunity to make a choice doesn't mean they have the knowledge and understanding to make an informed one. Parents still use TV as a baby-sitter, teenagers still learn conspicuous consumption from commercials, and adults still watch trivial game shows. For that to change, they all must become media literate.

The media literacy movement, though begun in Australia in the 1980s, has taken its greatest hold in Canada. U.S. media violence flows across Canada's borders unimpeded. In fact, 80 percent of the violence on Canadian television is picked up from U.S. programing. Canadians awoke in abrupt stages to the possibility of this violence stimulating real-life violence. They were jolted when fourteen young women were shot to death at the Ecole Polytechnique in Montreal in 1989, and again when thirteen-year-old Virginie Lariviere launched a national petition to ban all TV violence after her little sister was raped and strangled in 1991. By the time she presented her petition to the prime minister two years later, Lariviere had collected 1.3 million signatures.

Rather than banning TV violence, the Canadian government responded with a plan that stressed voluntary efforts on the part of writers, producers, advertisers, educators, and parents. One official described the approach as "consensual and cooperative, not legalistic and coercive." The government asked the Canadian Association of Broadcasters to revise its voluntary code, which it did, agreeing to ban excessive violence in dramas and music videos and to allow violence unsuited for children only after 9 P.M. Also, Canada's major advertisers were encouraged to withhold ads from violent shows. But most of the plan focused on increasing media literacy—on teaching media users, particularly children, to be more critically minded.

By 1998 just about every Canadian province had made media literacy a mandatory part of the school curriculum. John Pungente, who has lectured on media literacy throughout Canada and Australia, states that media literacy programs give students "an understanding of how media messages are constructed and how they influence values, beliefs and behaviour. . . . Common themes for discussion include the use of violence in conflict resolution, gender issues and racial stereotyping. Students also look at the financial base for media and popular entertainment." Researchers have confirmed that these activities make a difference. "The more that children think and talk about television and other media," Pungente sums up, "the less influence the media have on them."

Media literacy is recognized in Canada today as an essential outcome of education, like reading or writing. In the United States, by contrast, media literacy has made only weak and scattered progress. Why? Bok says it is because many Americans, exhibiting a culturally ingrained faith in the benefits of technology, believe that the V-chip will solve the issue of media violence for them. But the V-chip can't block out violent news, or model nonviolent behavior for children, or examine what kind of savage society considers violence entertaining in the first place.

ROCK ON

The Rock contains distinct echoes of several classic action films—the manhunt through sewers from *The Third Man* (1950), the car chase from *Bullitt* (1968), the slow-motion, Pollack-like blood splatters from *The Wild Bunch* (1969). After its enormous box-office success, *The Rock* itself became a model for still other action films—such as *Con Air* (1997), *Face/Off* (1997), and *Mission: Impossible 2* (2000)—which often featured even ghastlier and deadlier violence. Will the spiral ever end?

Probably not, according to media analysts. Jeffrey Goldstein points out that social and historical circumstances influence the popularity of violent entertainment. During wartime, or when violence plagues our communities, it rises in popularity. "Violent entertainment," Goldstein concludes, "may be as inevitable as violence in society."

Others have suggested that the attractions of violent entertainment are primarily psychological. Dolf Zillman, for example, notes that people become acclimated to the arousal produced by violent images, but that they continue to crave the excitement that viewing violence can bring. "Does this mean," he asks, "that we shall have to accept an ever-increasing utilization of violence and terror for entertainment purposes?" He thinks yes.

But where is the harm in that? Some analysts argue that there is none. In fact, Lawrence Jarvik claims that media depictions of violence not only reflect "a fundamental confidence in individual freedom and personal liberty," but also fulfill a civic function. "Repeated illustrations of violence and immorality," he comments, "are necessary to impart ethical lessons to the citizenry just as 'hellfire and brimstone' are used in sermons to emphasize the frightening prospects of hell."

Debate over the effects of media violence has raged a long time. The fear that violent images would corrupt filmgoers is nearly as old as film itself. In 1916 prominent psychologist Hugo Munsterberg published *The Photoplay: A Psychological Study* in which he warned, "The sight of crime and of vice may force itself on the consciousness with disastrous results. . . . The possibilities of psychical infection and destruction cannot be overlooked." His concerns would be repeated by educators, politicians, social workers, and other critics over the following decades. Just recently, Harvard doctoral student Fumie Yokota, whose research has found that many G-rated animated films contain a surprising amount of violence, expressed alarm about the message cartoon violence may be sending child viewers. "It may desensitize kids so much," Yokota states, "they think it's OK and no big deal for somebody to be smacked in the head with a hammer."

Most of the dire predictions made over the years about a steady diet of media violence leading to mental illness, juvenile delinquency, or real-life violence have yet to come true. Warnings like Munsterberg's now seem wildly overstated. The connections between things seen and things done have turned out to be more subtle and complex—and, in a way, even more far-reaching.

Media violence has become so common and accepted today that we who partake of it may not realize its full effects on us. Violent images are all around us all the time, a routine feature of our environment. A strong current of violence flows through the films and TV shows we watch, the newspapers we read, the computer games we play, and the sports events we attend. We can say, in extenuation, that this violence is largely symbolic—that it does little or no actual harm. There are many other societies in the world much worse than ours, where the violence is real and intransigent, and the dead are left for the dogs and vultures.

Still, a society that finds violence entertaining, and that even allows the entertainment industry to target children and adolescents with violent fare, may be lost in its own sort of moral darkness. Prolonged exposure to media violence has been shown in study after study to desensitize viewers. And a desensitized viewer is one less likely to recognize the rights and feelings of others or to think ethically about human relationships. The symbolic violence spreading like a toxic spill in our midst may not actually destroy life, but neither does it promote the love and joy we need to live.

QUESTIONS TO CONSIDER

1. Who should exercise primary responsibility for controlling the exposure of children and adolescents to media violence—parents, the government, or the entertainment industry? Would your choice change if only one parent in ten had an accurate understanding of the TV ratings system or if only two in five have the V-chip (the actual findings of a recent poll by the Annenberg Public Policy Center)? Justify your answer.

2. Imagine you have been selected by neighbors because of your knowledge and eloquence to ask the local school board to implement a media literacy program. Prepare a presentation that explains what exactly media literacy is, why it is needed in schools today, and how it is typically taught. Cite examples of media literacy efforts elsewhere to support your case.

3. Analyze a recent action film according to the nine factors identified by the National Television Violence Study as contributing to the effects of violence on viewers. Is violence depicted in such a way in the film as to increase the risk of viewers becoming desensitized, aggressive, or fearful?

4. Bok notes that because film critics are among "the most heavily exposed consumers" of entertainment violence, they run the risk of becoming hardened to appalling sights and losing touch with the reactions of ordinary filmgoers. Should critics take steps to prevent this occupational hazard from occurring? What might these be? Do media organizations have an ethical duty to help protect the critics from desensitization?

5. Describe the characteristics a media depiction of violence must possess in order to be considered ethical. Use examples from print, television, or film to illustrate your points.

FURTHER READING

Bok, Sissela. *Mayhem: Violence As Public Entertainment*. Reading, Mass.: Addison-Wesley, 1998.

Center for Media Literacy, <http://www.medialit.org

Dudley, William, ed. *Media Violence: Opposing Viewpoints.* San Diego, Calif.: Greenhaven, 1999.

Goldstein, Jeffrey, ed. *Why We Watch: The Attractions of Violent Entertainment.* New York: Oxford University Press, 1998.

Huber, Wolfgang. *Violence: The Unrelenting Assault on Human Dignity.* Trans. Ruth C. L. Gritisch. Minneapolis: Fortress, 1993.

Levine, Madeline. *Viewing Violence: How Media Violence Affects Your Child's and Adolescent's Development.* New York: Doubleday, 1996.

McGuckin, Frank, ed. *Violence in American Society.* New York: Wilson, 1998.

Medved, Michael. *Hollywood vs. America.* New York: HarperCollins, 1992.

Seabrook, John. *Nobrow: The Culture of Marketing—The Marketing of Culture.* New York: Knopf, 2000.

Starker, Steve. *Evil Influences: Crusades against the Mass Media.* New Brunswick, N.J.: Transaction, 1989.

Epilogue

The *Poughkeepsie Journal*, a chain-owned daily in upstate New York with folksy pretensions, publishes an occasional Sunday column called "You Be the Editor." The column describes the sort of ethical dilemmas that might occur in a newsroom and challenges readers to solve them. In one typical scenario, your education reporter wants to march in a pro-choice rally, arguing that abortion isn't part of her beat and so her participation doesn't represent a conflict of interest. In another, a photographer brings you a dead-body photo of a fifteen-year-old boy killed in the crossfire of a local gang war. Do you print it or not? Readers can send their responses to the *Journal*, which compares them in a later column to what actual editors say they would have done.

How useful is the exercise? At the very least, it gives readers some insight into the complexities of newspaper editing, as well as some sympathy for harried editors. "Newspaper editors," one recent column observes, "must be able to work quickly, but they must also be adept at discussing difficult questions from all angles, and at anticipating the impact of their decisions—all while deadlines loom." This is an accurate enough summary of how editors are expected to operate. Unfortunately, the expectations may be unrealistic and, in the end, a serious hindrance to ethical decision making.

If one consistent theme has emerged from the previous chapters, it is the need for journalists not to rush things into print or onto the air, not to automatically follow the precut grooves of customary practice, not to make snap decisions. Instead, they ought to slow down the pace of decision making and think beyond the seeming urgencies of the immediate moment. "I only know one guideline," Catholic philosopher Wolfgang Huber says, "that can give our conscience a better hearing when making decisions: slowness. I therefore describe the dilemma in which journalists find themselves daily as the conflict between the slowness of conscience and the quickness of actual events." He ruefully adds that quickness all too often wins out.

This should perhaps come as no surprise. The media in particular and modern life in general are increasingly defined by speed. Everything is quick, quick, quick. We have instant messenger, fast food, express lanes. What we don't have is a lot of patience for long drawn-out ethical reflection.

The "You Be the Editor" column presents ethics in a style nicely suited to today's short attention spans. It devotes just a paragraph apiece to four different newsroom situations that all demand a decisive response from the editor. Consciously or not, the column conceives of ethics as a form of crisis management. Readers are left with the impression that ethical dilemmas are extraordinary events that erupt without warning and in isolation from each other and that must be resolved on an ad hoc basis, preferably as quickly as possible.

Many media-ethics textbooks, by using the case-study approach, create the same impression—that ethical dilemmas are discontinuous, dramatic, and disruptive. The cases often seem to suggest that a concern for ethics lasts only as long as the dilemmas described in them do. Once a solution is devised—or, more accurately, improvised—and organizational routine is restored, ethical concerns again fade into the background, remaining there until the next storm strikes.

But a chief lesson of the films analyzed in this book is that we can't wait like Russell Price in *Under Fire* or Steve Everett in *True Crime* for a special situation to grip our hearts and finally inspire us to behave ethically. What happens if such a situation never arises? Ethics is about how we conduct ourselves day in and day out, particularly in regard to others. For media practitioners, this means that ethics should be woven directly into the fabric of their work, not be considered, as it now is, an emergency repair kit for fixing sudden rips in the fabric.

The ultimate character of a media outlet lies less in how it handles big flashy issues—invasion of privacy, entertainment violence, the use of secret sources—than in how it handles basic stuff: Are employees overworked and underpaid? Who decides the play of stories? Can the audience recognize itself in the content? These are the sorts of mundane questions by which the ethics of a newspaper or broadcast station can be measured. Textbooks notwithstanding, the vast majority of ethical decisions don't come accompanied by thunder and lightning. The vast majority come quietly, as part of the daily detail of media production. This, if anything, makes ethics even harder to do. It requires that media practitioners regularly exercise vigilance and empathy, develop the habit of caring.

Is this too much to ask of mere humans? In the films we watched, we met characters who overcome external obstacles or internal doubts, or both, to grow in ethics. Alicia Clark, the cost-conscious managing editor in *The Paper*, winds up ordering an eleventh-hour replate of the front page when she realizes, finally, that truth is more important than the bottom line. The jurors in *12 Angry Men* struggle through prejudice, class differences, and conflicting evidence to reach the right verdict. Even Chuck Tatum, the former star reporter who viciously exploits a trapped miner in *Ace in the Hole*, feels the stirrings of conscience in the end.

Of course, these are fictional situations, done up in heroic Hollywood style. Would actual people similarly rise to the occasion? What would be the cost if they didn't?

A glance back at a fact-based film, John Sayles's *Eight Men Out*, suggests that the cost would be terrible. The crooked ballplayers do harm not only to their team and the grand old game of baseball, but also to public faith in the truthfulness of appearances. The stain of the "Black Sox" scandal spreads beyond the championship series, beyond Chicago, beyond 1919, seeping into the larger world and forever darkening social relationships with despair and suspicion.

But the ballplayers aren't evil. They are tragic. They feel cheated by the team owner, so they cheat in turn. Later, as events slip out of their control, they realize that they have only compounded the original wrong by accepting the gamblers' money. They wish now that they had acted differently. They might have, too, if they had reflected more on the likely consequences of their actions before they acted.

It is something we ourselves need to do. We live suspended in a dimly etched web of roles and relationships. Our actions ripple through the web, setting off effects we can't always anticipate, can't always know or name. As media practitioners, we may be armed with the awesome power of modern communication technology, but as humans, we are small and fallible. Moral tragedy is never more than just one bad decision away. We should try to remember this whenever a deadline approaches, the pressure to publish or broadcast mounts, and the future of democracy seems at stake.

Filmography

ACE IN THE HOLE
1951, 111 minutes
Directed by Billy Wilder
Screenplay by Walter Newman, Lesser Samuels, and Billy Wilder
Chuck Tatum: Kirk Douglas
Lorraine Minosa: Jan Sterling
Jacob Q. Booth: Porter Hall
Leo Minosa: Richard Benedict
Herbie Cook: Robert Arthur

DEADLINE U.S.A.
1952, 87 minutes
Directed and written by Richard Brooks
Ed Hutcheson: Humphrey Bogart
Margaret Garrison: Ethel Barrymore
Nora Hutcheson: Kim Novak
Frank Allen: Ed Begley
Tomas Rienzi: Martin Gabel

12 ANGRY MEN
1957, 96 minutes
Directed by Sidney Lumet
Screenplay by Reginald Rose
Juror #3: Lee J. Cobb
Juror #4: E. G. Marshall
Juror #5: Jack Klugman
Juror #6: Ed Binns
Juror #7: Jack Warden
Juror #8: Henry Fonda
Juror #9: Joseph Sweeney
Juror #10: Ed Begley
Juror #11: George Voskovec
Juror #12: Robert Webber

ALL THE PRESIDENT'S MEN
1976, 138 minutes
Directed by Alan J. Pakula
Screenplay by William Goldman
Carl Bernstein: Dustin Hoffman
Bob Woodward: Robert Redford
Ben Bradlee: Jason Robards
Harry Rosenfeld: Jack Warden
Howard Simons: Martin Balsam
"Deep Throat": Hal Holbrook
Hugh W. Sloan Jr.: Stephen Collins

NETWORK
1976, 120 minutes
Directed by Sidney Lumet
Screenplay by Paddy Chayefsky
Max Schumacher: William Holden
Diana Christensen: Faye Dunaway
Howard Beale: Peter Finch
Frank Hackett: Robert Duvall
Arthur Jensen: Ned Beatty

UNDER FIRE
1983, 100 minutes
Directed by Roger Spottiswoode

Screenplay by Ronald Shelton and Clayton Frohman
Russell Price: Nick Nolte
Alex Grazier: Gene Hackman
Claire Stryder: Joanna Cassidy
Somoza: Rene Enriques
Jazy: Jean-Louis Trintignant
Herb Kittle: Richard Masur
Priest: Carlos Romano
Oates: Ed Harris

EIGHT MEN OUT
1988, 120 minutes
Directed and written by John Sayles
Buck Weaver: John Cusack
Charles Comiskey: Clifton James
Arnold Rothstein: Michael Lerner
Bill Burns: Christopher Lloyd
William "Kid" Gleason: John Mahoney
Oscar "Happy" Felsch: Charlie Sheen
Eddie Cicotte: David Strathairn
"Shoeless" Joe Jackson: D. B. Sweeney
Ray Schalk: Gordon Clapp
Arnold "Chick" Gandil: Michael Rooker
Charles "Swede" Risberg: Don Harvey
Billy Maharg: Richard Edson
Abe Attell: Michael Mantell
Joseph "Sport" Sullivan: Kevin Tighe
Ring Lardner: John Sayles
High Fullerton: Studs Terkel

THE PAPER
1994, 112 minutes
Directed by Ron Howard
Screenplay by David and Stephen Koepp
Henry Hackett: Michael Keaton
Bernie White: Robert Duvall
Alicia Clark: Glenn Close
Martha Hackett: Marisa Tomei
McDougal: Randy Quaid
Graham Keighley: Jason Robards

Marion Sandusky: Jason Alexander
Paul Bladden: Spalding Gray
Susan: Catherine O'Hara
Janet: Lynne Thigpen

THE ROCK
1996, 129 minutes
Directed by Michael Bay
Screenplay by David Weisberg, Douglas S. Cook, and Mark Rosner
Patrick Mason: Sean Connery
Stanley Goodspeed: Nicholas Cage
Gen. Francis X. Hummel: Ed Harris
Maj. Tom Baxter: David Morse
Capt. Hendrix: John C. McGinley
Sgt. Crisp: Bokeen Woodbine

TRUE CRIME
1999, 127 minutes
Directed by Clint Eastwood
Screenplay by Larry Gross, Paul Brickman, and Stephen Schiff
Steve Everett: Clint Eastwood
Frank Beachum: Isaiah Washington
Bob Findley: Denis Leary
Alan Mann: James Woods
Bonnie Beachum: Lisa Gay Hamilton
Barbara Everett: Diane Venora

Index

About the Authors

HOWARD GOOD is the coordinator of the Journalism Program at the State University of New York at New Paltz. He is the author of, among other works, *The Drunken Journalist*, *Girl Reporter*, and *The Journalist as Autobiographer*.

MICHAEL J. DILLON is a Professor of Communications at Duquesne University.